MASTERING
TECHNICAL ANALYSIS

M A S T E R I N G
TECHNICAL
ANALYSIS

Michael C. Thomsett

DEARBORN™
A **Kaplan Professional** Company

This publication is designed to provide accurate and authoritative information in regard to the subject matter covered. It is sold with the understanding that the publisher is not engaged in rendering legal, accounting, or other professional service. If legal advice or other expert assistance is required, the services of a competent professional person should be sought.

Editorial Director: Cynthia Zigmund
Managing Editor: Jack Kiburz
Project Editor: Trey Thoelcke
Interior Design: Lucy Jenkins
Cover Design: DePinto Studios
Typesetting: Eliot House Productions

Published by Dearborn
A Kaplan Professional Company

Printed in the United States of America

99 00 01 10 9 8 7 6 5 4 3 2 1

Library of Congress Cataloging-in-Publication Data
Thomsett, Michael C.
  Mastering technical analysis / Michael C. Thomsett.
     p.   cm.
  Includes index.
  ISBN 0-7931-3359-9 (pbk.)
  1. Investment analysis. 2. Stocks—Prices Charts, diagrams, etc. I. Title.
HG4529.T493   1999   99–37991
332.63'222—dc21   CIP

CONTENTS

PREFACE

Your investment decisions are only as good as the information on which those decisions are based. This seemingly obvious point bears repeating over and over, because one of the more serious flaws in many investment strategies is the flaw of forgetting to constantly review information.

Long-term investors often base their approach to the selection of stocks and timing of sales on a belief that the fundamentals should rule. These include financial statements issued by the subject corporation as well as interim reports, historical financial trends, and forecasts concerning future growth, sales, and profits. Even those investors who follow faithfully the idea of fundamental analysis easily can fall into the all too common trap of responding to other indicators, such as index movements, rumors, and short-term changes in stock prices. These are valid indicators in perspective, but are they enough to make important investment decisions?

Technical analysis is nothing like fundamental analysis. Instead of depending on historical financial information, the technician believes that changes in stocks and in the market itself can be judged based on recent trends in stock price changes, the relationship between price and earnings, the volume of activity in a particular stock or industry, and other similar indicators. While the fundamental investor bases decisions on historical changes in financial strength, the technician depends on more immediate market-related trends—stock price changes reflected in charts, the shape of chart movements, volume and volatility indicators, and index changes, to name a few.

Which approach works better cannot be said, because both techniques have merit. The purpose of this book is to demonstrate the range of technical indicators and to provide you with practical methods for incorporating those indicators into your individual program for analysis. Several useful tools are employed to aid you in this, including:

- *Graphs and charts.* Technical analysis is based on the study of price movement trends (among other factors), which requires extensive study of price charts and volume within stocks and industry groups. This book uses many graphs and charts to aid in making information clear and visual.
- *Examples.* To clarify points, few techniques work as well as the use of applicable examples. This book attempts to show how theories can be applied in the real world of the stock market, and how outcomes may vary from one person to another, requiring different response strategies.
- *Definitions.* The stock market is daunting for even experienced investors because of the specialized jargon and lingo used by insiders. While the unique language of Wall Street might be convenient for those who work there every day, it also isolates the average individual investor. As ideas are introduced throughout the book, definitions are included in context; these also are summarized in the extensive glossary at the end of the book.
- *Key points.* Another handy tool to help you as you go along is the use of key points. These are highlighted throughout the book in sidebars. You can work your way through the book, reading only the key points, and gain an overview of the flow of information, pausing to read further when needed. In this way, the key points are excellent guides for particular subject areas.
- *Walk-throughs.* Step-by-step summaries of methods and techniques help you to grasp the idea of the moment without trouble. In comparison, an overly complex narrative explanation might require far more work to comprehend.

These tools are intended to help you master the most useful aspects of technical analysis. There is no area of investing too complex to be comprehended and mastered by the typical investor. *Mastering Technical Analysis* is designed with this idea in mind and speaks to the average investor rather than the student, the professional Wall Street trader, or the highly specialized technician. It will simplify and explain rather than confuse; it will demonstrate and pose alternatives rather than assume one outcome and move ahead from there. The book is meant to help you gain insights and understanding.

INTRODUCTION

Analysis or Guesswork?

The selection of an individual stock or industry group can be a highly personalized or rigidly formulated process. The decision about how to make decisions in the market is up to you. The most important fact to remember is that there is no one "right way" to always decide when to buy, to hold, or to sell.

Some decision-making techniques are effective in a given set of circumstances, but might not work well in all situations. Immediate market news could make a time-consuming and methodical approach impractical, and sudden changes in the financial condition of a company could mean that careful study and analysis are required before any decision should be made. People go wrong when they adopt one procedure for making investment decisions, without developing an understanding of what the information really provides; how such information can be applied to a given situation; and whether a particular decision based on the information fits within the individual plan—including financial goals, risk tolerance level, financial position, and other qualifying points.

Another time that problems arise is when investors find themselves trying to outguess the market. They want to find ways to recognize what will happen before everyone else. This is an impossible task and often conflicts with personal investing goals. For example, many people begin with long-term goals, such as saving for retirement, for buying a home, or for a child's college education. They recognize the importance of building a long-term portfolio. When it comes to making investment decisions, however, they fall into the trap of acting like short-term specula-tors—trading too often, going for fast profits, and forgetting that the real goal is to build profitable investments into a portfolio.

Working on guesswork defeats the purpose of attempting to devise methods for analysis. The reason for studying technical analysis (or fundamental analysis) is to eliminate as much uncer-tainty as possible, to reduce risks, and to increase your chances for profit. Unless you are, indeed, a speculator and you want to go in and out of investments from day to day seeking fast profits, you probably need to stay away from short-term strategies. This is obvious, but often ignored, advice. Guesswork actually may defeat your purpose by leading you into ill-advised and overly speculative investments rather than into decisions that will help you to reach your long-term investing goals.

You can use technical analysis techniques to improve your forecasting ability, not only in the selection of corporations whose stock is likely to rise in the future, but for avoiding the common problems investors make. Business forecasting and investment forecasting have some important similarities as well as differences, and being aware of these attributes will help you to select techniques and hone skills designed to improve your stock selection abilities.

Among the similarities, the most important is that forecasting always involves trying to estimate future outcomes. It is an imperfect science because it is rarely precise. In business, the purpose is to pose a series of outcomes that seem reasonable (in sales volume, for example), and then to study the probable effect on costs, expenses, and profits. Business forecasting also involves anticipating capital improvement, staffing, and facility requirements to support growth, among other planning require-ments. In investing, forecasting takes on a different purpose. By trying to estimate future stock price levels, investors want to pick the stocks with the greatest price growth potential. A reality often overlooked about this is the correlation between growth potential and risk. As a general rule, the greater the growth potential, the greater the market risk (as well as other forms of risk), and vice versa. So in selecting stocks with a range of potential, you also need to be aware of your own willingness to undertake risk—how much, how soon, and how often.

Business forecasting normally involves gross sales volume, whereas investment forecasting typically is limited to stock price. Forecasting also includes dividend payments, sales and profit volume, and related financial outcomes. The real test of a stock's success, however, invariably returns to the stock price: What did you pay for it and what is it worth today?

Technical analysis can be employed to help recognize emerging changes in market strength, weakness, enthusiasm, volume, support for stock price levels, and more—in other words, to take the temperature of the market. Fundamental analysis, which is the study of historical financial results and of forecasts for sales and profits, is largely financial in nature, whereas technical analysis is more concentrated on market forces, such as supply and demand for stock, price strength and resistance, chart patterns, and predictions about the next price direction.

Some so-called technical indicators are gimmicks that provide you with nothing of value, and even a preliminary honest analysis will prove that point. Of greater value are those technical indicators that can be used to judge market strengths and weaknesses: support for current price ranges of stocks, status of an industry group and how that may affect stock prices, volatility and volume, and the relationship between fundamental and technical analysis.

It is the selection of "smart" technical indicators that will distinguish you from less astute investors, from those who follow the herd and, rather than making individual decisions, are content to do what everyone else is doing. As a smart technical investor, you will be able to recognize the real meaning that can be taken from emerging technical trends, and to combine technical and fundamental information so that the information available to you can be used to make tough decisions. This can be achieved without having to become highly analytical, without having to master very specialized skills involving higher math and detailed financial expertise, and without needing to hire someone just to tell you what the numbers mean.

Technical analysis is not so complicated that most people can't make good use of it. By simply defining your terms and defining a limited number of indicators of greatest value to you, it is possible to devise an intelligent strategy. This will help you to make informed decisions, identify potentially profitable stocks, respect your own risk tolerance limits, and recognize changes in trends before it is too late.

CHAPTER 1

Cycles in Investing

All of investing is about cycles—the unending tendency of events to move upward and downward, to be alternatively positive and negative, optimistic and pessimistic, good and bad. Cycles are devices that describe this tendency and that can be used to predict, track, and recognize cyclical movements.

For example, stock prices might be predictable, at least to some degree, based on the predictability of one or more related cycles—of price trends, seasonal volume, profitability, or industry, for example. Of course, other factors, such as the overall market conditions, corporate financial performance and management, and the perceived future value of the stock, all influence the stock price. However, because cycles accurately reflect up-and-down changes, a premise within technical analysis is that

KEY POINT

Cycles can be used to attempt to predict future stock price movements, because cycles establish a rhythm of up-and-down change.

1

the cycle of investing can be utilized to predict future stock price movements.

To begin, let us define *technical analysis*. It is the study of stock prices and related matters, involving analysis of recent and historical price trends and cycles. The technician also studies factors beyond stock price, such as dividend payments, trading volume, index trends, industry group trends and popularity, and volatility of a stock. We will examine these technical indicators later on.

In comparison to technical analysis, investors also follow financial information with great interest. This activity is called *fundamental analysis*, which is the study of recent and historical financial results of a corporation for the purpose of forecasting future investment value.

Business and Investing Cycles

The term *cycle* is used widely in business to describe predictable changes that occur in a pattern. The timing of such changes varies greatly from one cycle to another, and it is sometimes difficult to recognize the place in a cycle at the moment. Often, cyclical changes and positions are clear only when reviewed from afar. When this limitation is applied to the desire for predicting stock price movements, it makes the process more interesting. Because you cannot always predict the *timing* of change, the cycle may be predictable, but the exact moment for decision cannot be known with certainty.

Saying that cycles demonstrate "predictable changes," does not mean to imply that you can know in advance when a stock's price will rise or fall. This only means that cycles occur in specific patterns over time. You can never know when cycle changes are going to occur, which direction a stock's price will move in interim changes, or how long a specific segment of the cycle will take. It could be days, weeks, or even years. That is what makes investing so interesting. A well-selected investment might indeed pay off, but you have no way of knowing how long it will take.

KEY POINT

Uncertainty is the most challenging part of investing—and the most interesting.

The uncertainty of timing is what makes investing so challenging. You can understand cycles with great depth, but when it comes to knowing when to take action, you are in the same quandary as everyone else: Acting too soon, you lose opportunities; waiting too long, you miss opportunities.

Business cycles and investing cycles share the same characteristics, as do all cycles. But the elements are not the same. In the business cycle, emphasis is placed on matters such as sales, profits, market share, and budgetary controls, to name a few. It is perhaps ironic that these factors should influence investment decisions and the value of stocks, and in the real world they do not. While business cycles depend on the conduct of business, competition, the market, and the economy, the investment cycle does not. It depends almost solely on the *perception* of future value. Thus, in the auction marketplace where stocks are bought and sold, the perception of future value has complete influence on today's stock prices, sometimes in spite of contrary corporate indications.

These differences have much to do with the way that you use technical indicators, and with the way that you develop an analysis

KEY POINT

Business cycles rely on financial, marketing, and economic influences, whereas investing cycles depend largely on investors' perceptions about the stock's future value.

program for yourself that incorporates technical analysis. It would be nice if stock values would rise or fall solely based on the strength of corporate earnings power, the quality and talent of corporate management, position within a competitive environment, and quality of products and services. In fairness, every investor needs to acknowledge a contradiction in the way the market works. For long-term investment holdings, the selection of strong, well-managed, and financially secure companies is of utmost importance; the long-term value of a stock investment depends on consistency in management, well thought out business plans, and intelligent strategies in a competitive market. With the proper attributes and financial strength in place, corporate value does grow over the long term. For the more immediate analysis of stock prices, however, these fundamental attributes have little to do with stock prices and, in fact, do not stand up to the more immediate perception of a stock's future value.

This is troubling to anyone whose faith in fundamental analysis is deep. If you believe that the study of a corporate financial statement is a suitable guide for the selection of stock, then the immediate market factors are contradictory. We all have seen examples of this. Many initial public offerings are so immediately in demand that the company's stock price rises dramatically, to the point that the stock's value far exceeds book value of the company. The stock of the Internet bookstore Amazon.com is a case in point. During a period of years in which no profits were earned, Amazon.com's stock rose from quarter to quarter in dramatic fashion. On what basis? Without any history of corporate profits, why was the stock in demand?

That is the question the fundamental analyst would ask; however, the technician recognizes the answer: It is the *perception* of future value that determines today's stock prices. The stock market reacts to the forces of supply and demand in pure form, meaning that logic and fundamental information might have nothing to do with price movements.

In the study of cycles, supply and demand is the driving force for all changes. It is the engine that makes the cycle move from one phase to another. In the business cycle, supply and demand is

KEY POINT

Price movement is determined independently from the more logical and historical perspective of fundamental analysis. Prices change because of perceptions about the future, whereas the fundamentals report on the past.

reflected in competitive change, in how quickly or slowly products move from warehouse to shelf to consumer, and in how much influence is exerted by the forces that help or hurt profits—the regulatory sector of the government, competitors, employees and unions, and customers.

In business, the forces of supply and demand change constantly. Business managers are constantly involved in forecasting. They forecast sales, expenses, profits, market share, and every other financial and nonfinancial aspect of business. Forecasts always are based on basic assumptions about the future, which grow from what is known today. Because the future never comes out exactly as expected, forecasts are invariably flawed in some way, so they have to be revised constantly. The supply and demand variances within the business cycle make forecasting elusive, but also wonderfully interesting. Accounting departments of large companies spend major effort in attempting to pin down future movements of dollars and cents, and executives attempt to outguess the market by trying to recognize market forces before the competition does.

KEY POINT

The most interesting thing about forecasting is that it is never accurate; it is always based on today's knowledge, which is almost always wrong when applied to the future.

In business, forecasting often is based largely on a detailed analysis of information and historical trends. This reliance on the historical does help to improve forecasting abilities, but even with the most detailed analysis, the forecast is rarely accurate enough to be relied on. The real value of the business forecast is in the way it is used, if used properly. Executives use forecasts to anticipate future needs and to fill them efficiently and in ways that maintain and increase future profits. This involves management of cash flow, capital investment, employment levels, inventory, competition, and an unending variety of other business factors.

The investing cycle is not the same as the business cycle, a reality often ignored or misunderstood by investors. When you are trying to anticipate near-term price movements, it is important to recognize that business factors (such as sales and profits) are *not* going to influence stock prices. Too many investors assume that such factors are at play in short-term price changes, and that simply is not the case. To investigate this claim, you may analyze a stock's price movement in comparison with interim corporate reports.

Financial outcome does influence stock value in some respects, often in ways that are not logical. As was previously stated, long-term stock value depends on solid financial and corporate management; but in the short term, this is not always the case. It is more likely that stock prices will be influenced by outcomes at variance with prior predictions.

> **Example:** A particular company's listed stock sells for $54 per share. A quarterly earnings report was published this morning, showing profits of $1.35 per share. The prediction for this quarter's earnings was made three months ago at $1.50 per share. As a consequence of the lower-than-expected earnings, the stock falls three points.

The example above is not atypical. In financial terms, the $1.35 earnings per share might be dazzling in the minds of corporate management. But if the Wall Street analyst predicted $1.50, the outcome is disappointing. It also should be noted that a higher-than-expected outcome would be expected to have the opposite effect on the stock's price.

The $1.50 prediction for earnings per share represents the market's expectation of future value. It is an opinion and an estimate and has nothing to do with financial performance. Remember, that financial results are reports about the past. The analysis of a corporation's potential is always forward looking and, to the extent that past financial outcome is used, predictions will make a certain amount of sense. But on Wall Street, the analysis of future income is a judgment of potential. Any prediction about future earnings per share cannot possibly be related to past performance. Remember, when you are looking forward but basing your estimates on what occurred in the past, an estimate is of dubious value. Because perception is all-important in the market, however, the comparison between predicted and actual outcome has everything to do with the value of stock.

The illogic of this is the reality that investors face, and it is particularly difficult for anyone with a financial background to digest. In terms of profits earned per share, for example, it is apparent that an acceptable level of performance might have a natural ceiling, and it would be unrealistic to expect profits to climb beyond that ceiling indefinitely. In the forecasting game, however, it is a requirement that future performance be better— higher, more profitable—than past performance. It might be impractical or even unhealthy for a corporation to strive for such an outcome, but the analyst requires growth in order to offer a positive forecast. Thus, much of the negative Wall Street news is short term in nature, because a drop in stock price resulting from a disappointing earnings report often is very temporary.

KEY POINT

Expectations of ever-increasing improvement in financial results often are unrealistic and might distort analysis of a company's investment value.

This is valuable information. Knowing that such reports and the resulting changes in stock prices are temporary in their effect, you may be able to play investment cycles against business cycles and profit as a result—speculative, to be sure, but often profitable.

What does this mean? How can you play one cycle against another? Supply and demand in investing is very different from supply and demand in business. Thus, the analytical study of a corporation's quarterly earnings affects stock prices only insofar as they exceed or fall short of an analyst's prediction (in the most immediate terms only). Knowing this, you may recognize a short-term buying opportunity when a stock's value falls, or a short-term selling opportunity when a stock's value rises more than was predicted.

Supply and demand in business depends on market and competitive factors. But in the stock market, it is almost always perception of value that makes a stock's price rise or fall. Thus, a study of business cycles and the prediction of those outcomes can be used to improve your investing know-how. Simply put, a stock's price rises when there are more buyers than sellers; it falls when there are more sellers than buyers. The more interesting question you might ask is, "Why are there more of one than the other set?" The answer, you will find, is that stocks tend to rise or fall—and the mix of buyers and sellers tends to change—as the direct result of immediate perceptions, to a far greater degree than any fundamental information would dictate.

It is not the similarities between business cycles and investing cycles that present opportunities, as most investors believe; rather, it is the differences that can provide you with the insights to outperform the market.

KEY POINT

Comparisons between business cycles and investing cycles might point to opportunities that most investors do not recognize.

Cycles and Prediction

By watching cycles, you can predict the likely direction of movement of a stock's price. But the cycle does not tell you everything, including these three points: It does not ensure accuracy; it does not ensure that interim opposing movements will not occur; and it does not help with timing.

1. *Accuracy.* Cycles are only predictive tools. They are not guaranteed, and past movement by no means demonstrates beyond any doubt what will take place in the future. You also cannot rely on the degree of change that might occur in the future. With investing, hindsight is always better than foresight; so cycles might indicate the likely future price movement direction—but this is not always right, nor is the level of change easily identified.

KEY POINT

Cycles are useful as predictive tools, but should not be depended on as a "sure thing" for making future investment decisions.

2. *Interim changes.* You might assume, based on past cyclical movements, that a stock's price is going to rise in the future. You might be right. But in between the present and the unidentified future, many things could occur, including a fall in price level. In that respect, a well-managed company's stock reasonably can be assumed to be on a long-term upward trend, based on many factors, including its price cycles of the past. That does not mean, however, that the positive change is going to happen this week, or even this year.

KEY POINT

It is reasonable to forecast price increases for well-managed companies. Eventually, you will be right; but your concern has to be in identifying the most likely price changes during the immediate future.

3. *Timing.* The most troubling aspect of cycles is timing. You easily can predict a price increase for a stock at some point in the future, and you might be right if you are willing to wait long enough. However, for the hundreds of stocks that will increase in market value at some future point, *when* will those changes occur? This is the tough part. Investors are not dependent on cycles for the direction of price movement alone. It is most common to ask, "Will this stock rise in value?" Of far greater importance to investors, though, is the question, "When will the price change?"

KEY POINT

Timing is everything. If you were able, in advance, to identify with certainty when stock prices would rise or fall, you wouldn't need any analysis whatsoever, just a larger bag for taking your money to the bank.

Prediction in business is a matter of forecasting and budgeting. Based on the past, and on a study of the mix of income, costs, and expenses, a competent accountant can put together a convincing argument showing one likely outcome for the future. The value of this process is that it provides a general guideline for the coming year. Actual results can be compared against the budgetary guideline as a means for judging how well the company is managing its income, controlling costs and expenses, and causing profits to be earned.

In comparison to investment prediction, the business task is relatively simple. The function of accounting budgets is to monitor, track, and control. The purpose of investment prediction is to judge when and where to invest money. While the accounting task enables management to spot and reverse negative trends, investors might find themselves in a loss position suddenly and without any signs. That is why different types of skills have to be applied by investors.

Unlike the accounting budget, the investment prediction has to be based on indicators that emerge from day to day and month to month, any one of which might change an opportunity drastically and suddenly. The technician who also watches the fundamentals uses a mix of information, both financial and market oriented; the absolute technician depends almost exclusively on cycles of one or more types.

How does the investor actually predict future price movement of a stock? Because the stock market is operated as an auction marketplace, the force of supply and demand determines the answer to that question. The auction marketplace is entirely at the mercy of that market. If there are more buyers (demand), prices go up, and if there are more sellers (supply), prices weaken and fall. This is the reality of the stock market. That does not mean that price movement is not predictable. It does mean that the real key to price movement prediction is found in an understanding of the supply and demand cycle.

If you are able to identify and understand the force of supply and demand—as it relates to price movement in the market—

KEY POINT

Because the stock market is an auction marketplace, the supply and demand cycle determines price movement. This is the key to technical analysis.

then you can better understand how price movement occurs. You still cannot control the degree, timing, and aberrations of cyclical movements, but you can identify the elements that drive the cycle itself. Technical analysis is nothing more than a study of the various cyclical elements that affect price movement. Putting it another way, technical analysis is the study of the stock market's supply and demand cycle.

That cycle consists of many elements, which collectively add up to the sum total of the supply and demand in the market: new high/new low statistics, volume, volatility, charting, odd lot trading, index trends, and more—all of these indicators are portions or variations of the market's supply and demand status.

Forecasting Cycle Duration

The most intriguing and difficult task in cycle watching is prediction. This is true for all cycles and in all markets. It is fair to say that, given enough time, any reasonably well selected investment will be profitable. You cannot afford to be lax on this topic, however, because the timing of cycles makes a difference between profit and loss. The limitations of capital often require you to move funds from one stock to another because more promising opportunities present themselves. That does not mean the original investment was bad, only that you timed the cycles poorly.

If timing were not an issue in investing, we simply could find any of the hundreds of well-capitalized and well-managed corporations whose stock is publicly listed, place money randomly, and

KEY POINT

One of the most severe forms of loss in the market is opportunity loss—by leaving funds in stocks not yet ripe, you miss the opportunity to maximize profits elsewhere.

then wait for the profits to roll in. This method, incidentally, is not uncommon. It leaves much to be desired, however, because industries and specific companies have their own cycles, too—in terms of profitability, price, and popularity.

Profitability

Profitability is the most apparent factor affecting long-term cycle movement of the stock, but, oddly enough, it is not related directly to price movement. The profitability of a company might have little or no short-term effect on price for several reasons. First, if analysts' predictions are met, it generally is believed that the current price already reflects the expectation of profits. Second, market factors (e.g., supply and demand) sometimes are affected not by current profits as much as by the expectation of future profits, and the two are not the same thing. Third, whether we like it or not, price movements of a stock—market forces—very often have absolutely nothing to do with profitability—fundamentals—of the stock and the company.

KEY POINT

A stock's price movement is directly related not to the company's profits, but to market expectation about *future* profitability and potential.

Price

Price is often misunderstood in the market. A stock's current price reflects (in a general sense) the current agreed-on market value between buyers and sellers. The current market price is the price that sellers are willing to pay and the price at which sellers are willing to sell. But that is not all. Price also reflects a far more significant investment principle and a supply and demand market principle: Today's price reflects the opinion of the market at large about future potential. The price summarizes the belief in the market about potential future growth of the company.

This is best seen in light of the *price-earnings ratio* (PE), a comparison between the current market price of the stock and the earnings per share reported during the last reporting period. It is an odd ratio because it is one of the few that combines market (or technical) information with financial (or fundamental) information. The PE is especially useful as a means for studying stocks and value, because it is a summary of earnings multiples reflected in current market price. So when a PE is eight, that means the current price is eight times greater than current earnings per share. This means that the current price level represents a general belief that future potential earnings and growth for the company is that much greater than today's earnings level.

Ironically, investors are consistently wrong in their judgments about stock values based on PE, which is valuable information for long-term investing. The general belief is that low PE stocks do not represent good long-term investments, whereas high PE stocks do. However, numerous long-term studies demonstrate that low PE stocks outperform the market, whereas exceptionally high PE stocks underperform.[*]

KEY POINT

Investors are wrong consistently about stock values based on the price-earnings ratio. But the truly amazing thing is that, with this information in hand, investors do not change their behavior.

---

[*] Sanjoy Basu, 1977 study of 500 New York Stock Exchange issues over 14 months. This study confirmed an earlier finding by David Dremen of 1,200 stocks from 1968 to 1977. Additional analysis may be found in *Mastering Fundamental Analysis* (Dearborn, 1998), pp. 26–27, 32–36.

Popularity

Popularity is the final consideration in this analysis, and perhaps the most perplexing. The popularity of a particular stock or of its industry is worthy of some study. A stock or industry can come into popularity or fall out of it for no apparent reason, and certainly for no reason connected to the fundamentals, supply and demand cycles, or a particular market-related factor. It simply occurs. The stock market is illogical, and when it reacts it often overreacts to the news of the day. By the same argument, the preference for a particular type of stock in today's market is based largely on a perception of potential—often without any underlying cause or justification.

KEY POINT

Be aware of enthusiasm. That, by itself, is not enough to ensure that you will do better than the average. Many enthusiastic investors have lost money by selecting stocks for the wrong reasons.

Popularity is not always as illogical as this, but when illogic is the rule, there is also a tendency for stocks rise or fall in value far beyond the current technical or fundamental indication of their value. As an astute technician, you might identify opportunities when this occurs. For example, if a new issue climbs so high that its PE is far beyond any possible potential future earnings, only the highest risk takers should be buying. True, many people make significant profits from unjustified hysteria. But remember that such situations invariably are followed by an even more severe and rapid fall. The same arguments can be made when stocks fall in market price without good reason. When a stock's market value falls below even its book value, for example, that is an obvious buying opportunity.

When stocks move higher or lower in the extreme, that is an opportunity. Markets invariably overreact.

The popularity of investments, if not watched carefully, can create high risks for the inexperienced speculator. A good example is the unrealistic run-up in the price of gold during the late 1970s and early 1980s. Gold ran up to over $800 per ounce, only to fall to below $400 in a short time, where it has remained since. How many people invested in multiple ounces of gold at or above $800? The answer is that many did, because the false popularity of gold created artificial demand. Such demand can only last so long. When the market corrected, the price fell rapidly.

Artificial demand is temporary and often difficult to recognize. When it corrects, it does so quickly—and expensively.

Those who invested in gold at $800 per ounce learned an important and expensive lesson: When you invest in momentary enthusiasm (also known as greed), and without any underlying justification, the results often will be very expensive.

Popularity is a dangerous factor in the cycle. Because supply and demand is always at work and constantly playing back and forth, it is not unusual that false indicators (such as temporary artificial demand) are created. You might mistake such moments for indications that markets are about to take off, when in fact they might only be glitches in an otherwise stable or lackluster market. These matters are recognized easily in hindsight, during that period of time when your investment capital has been committed and might be gone.

Various Cyclical Forms

Every cycle is different. This, of course, makes it impossible to accurately judge how the market or a particular stock might act in the future. As will be shown in Chapter 5, there are some very valuable techniques involved in the charting of stock prices and volume, but it is unrealistic to expect that the timing and degree of price movement can be predicted with accuracy—given the nature of cycles.

A starting point is to recognize that price movement of stocks is itself cyclical. Some investors, particularly fundamentalists, struggle to avoid this conclusion. To those who follow the underlying financial data of a company, it seems only logical that growth in profits should lead to growth in the stock's market value. On a long-term basis, this usually is true. In the more attractive and exciting short term and even in the intermediate term, however, price movement often is unrelated to long-term profitability.

As a company's profits grow, the expectation of future price appreciation is reflected in changes in the stock's price. That is to say, consistently well-managed and profitable companies see increases in the market value of their stock, while poorly managed and unprofitable companies see decreases in the market value of their stock. That is a basic rule of thumb. Market perception is tied to value, which is a factor of future growth and profits.

With all of that in mind, the fundamentalist is frustrated because his analysis tells him only what *should* happen today and tomorrow. Market forces, however, really are not interested in long-term dependability of profits. Those forces cause more immediate changes in supply and demand, meaning that immediate price movement reflects perceptions of value even when the financial data show that such perceptions are not supported.

KEY POINT

Because perception and reality sometimes are at variance, the astute technician is able to develop an eye for opportunity.

In comparison, the technician has a different problem. She is more interested in the nature and causes of price movement, but really does not pay attention to the fundamentals. She already has realized that fundamentals are not useful for short-term prediction. Perhaps they should be, but in the real world of the market, they are not. This reality—frustrating to the fundamentalist—remains the truth. So the technician is aware that it is not the balance sheet, but the market forces at work today that determine whether the stock's price goes up or down tomorrow and next week.

This presents an entirely different set of analytical problems. The fundamentalist is able to apply a series of tests to determine the overall strength and safety of a company. The technician depends instead on a vast array of market forces. If a large mutual fund buys all available shares of a particular company, the company's stock price will rise, because there will be less supply out there for everyone else. It is also true that if the same fund dumps its large holdings in a particular company, an excess will be created in the supply and cause the price to fall. While these changes may be temporary, the actions of the fund's management

KEY POINT

We need to make a clear distinction between short-term price movement and long-term profit potential. They are confused easily when the decision point comes around.

have much more short-term impact on the stock's value than something as mundane as profit and loss.

It is ironic that some arguments made at the point of buying or selling stock have little or nothing to do with the *reasons* to buy or sell. For example, if you are thinking of selling a stock because it rose 30 percent in the past week and you want to take profits, a broker might argue that the company is well managed and may have significant long-term profits. That is a fundamental argument presented in a technical situation (the exceptionally large percentage run-up in price). The cycles that affect the price of stocks might exhibit different behaviors, even when a pattern repeats in the same issue from one year to the next. At times, stock prices roll gently upward in a gradual wave-like action, cresting higher after each quarterly report; at other times, stock prices (perhaps even for the same company) will move in jagged, random, and extreme patterns. It might be that the underlying fundamentals are the same, that popularity levels are not noticeably different, and that the popularity of the industry hasn't changed. Why, then, do all cycles behave differently?

The answer is that a variety of factors affect the nature of cycles. They are at least partially random; the actions of institutional investors (like mutual funds) often have a lot of effect on stock prices, especially if those funds move in and out of issues more frequently than they usually do. Changes in a company's management, insider trading, subsequent issue of new shares, repurchase and retirement of stock by the company, and general conditions in the market—all of these and more can and do affect

KEY POINT

The unpredictability of cyclical patterns is the only constant. Every cycle is different, even when the underlying causes and effects appear the same.

the pattern of price movement. This is true even when the moving average of the stock does not change.

The cycle, we need to remember, exists because supply and demand are fluid. They change with time and perception; they expand and contract. But neither the auction marketplace nor the supply and demand features driving create cycles. Instead, cycles are only one characteristic of the market environment. The same is true for many other environments: our physical bodies, our moods, the weather, and the change in the seasons, for example. Cycles represent the inertia of the market. Without cycles, supply and demand would remain constant, and so would prices. It is difficult to imagine a market in which supply and demand do not change. By definition, such an environment would not be a market at all.

KEY POINT

The nature of the market—of all markets—is change, and cycles represent those changes. Cycles are not independent features, but characteristics of the auction marketplace.

As you analyze stock price movement, hindsight is of little real value because you see only yesterday's opportunities, many or most of which you probably missed. However, once you begin to understand the elusive nature of cycles, what they represent and how and why no two cycles are the same, you will develop valuable insights into the nature of supply and demand and the workings of the market.

Rules of Thumb for Cycle Forecasting

Following are ten general rules of thumb worth remembering when studying the technical indicators of the stock market:

1. *Cycles might be more influenced by larger institutional investors than by the combined sentiment of individuals.* The stock market consists of two general segments: institutional investors (mutual funds, pension plan management, insurance companies, etc.) and retail investors (individuals). While there are many more individuals in the market, institutions collectively represent the vast majority of the dollars in the market. As a direct result, institutional investors have more control over cyclical movement, actual prices of stocks, and, to a degree, the varying levels of supply and demand—all because of their vast holdings in comparison to individual investors.

    What does this mean? It tells you that your individual actions within the market have less influence than the decisions made by large institutional managers. Your primary market advantage is mobility. It is difficult for institutional investors to make decisions and move funds quickly, just because of their size. This problem is apparent in results. In the latest full year studied (1997), only 10 percent of all mutual funds did better than the market average.* Part of the problem is that mutual funds represent so much of the total market that their result should approximate the median return. Considering that funds are professionally managed, however, it seems reasonable to expect that a higher percentage would show results *above* average.

KEY POINT

Big institutional investors have more influence in the market than individuals. But that does not mean that they do better, just that they are bigger.

---

* Morningstar, Inc., studies diversified stock funds each year. Performance results are dismal even during bull market periods. Only 24 percent of funds beat market averages in 1994; 16 percent in 1995; 26 percent in 1996; and only 10 percent in 1997.

2. *Prediction and forecasting in the market are not reliable, and there are no guarantees.* Some investors make the very basic error of believing that it is possible to predict market and price movement with some degree of reliability. In fact, a forecast is at best an educated guess. Those familiar with business forecasting make the mistake of believing that stock market forecasting is similar. In truth, business forecasting is relatively scientific and can be done reliably because corporations can exercise a degree of control over their own profits and losses. The same is not true in the market.

   Use cyclical analysis as one of many tools for improving your ability to judge market sentiment and conditions; but avoid the mistake of looking for a "sure thing" in the market environment, where nothing is certain except uncertainty, and where overreaction to all news is the norm.

KEY POINT

Business managers have some control over the accuracy of their forecasts, but investors can only hope that their timing and selection criteria are accurate, at least most of the time.

3. *Business forecasting and investment market forecasting are vastly different.* As mentioned previously, there are important differences between business forecasting and investment forecasting. In business, the forecast and budget are prepared based on historical data and on the development of a series of assumptions about what elements will effect the same outcomes in the future. In fact, business forecasting is fairly reliable when prepared correctly. If the assumption base for income is reasonable, then it also is reasonable to extrapolate a rate of growth based on recent trends.

You cannot use the same logic in the stock market. Some chartists attempt to study past price movement patterns to guess the next price direction. Charting has value, but it is limited because it attempts to predict future prices based on patterns, in a market that might be largely random. The value of charting is in recognizing likely ranges of results based on visible support and resistance levels (more on this in Chapter 5). Recognize that business forecasting is more scientific than any attempt to forecast a stock's price movement. There are technical analysis tools that can be used to improve your educated guess, but you will not find any sure things through price forecasting.

KEY POINT

Whether we like it or not, we cannot predict future price movement consistently. Investing is not like a business where sales levels can be caused by specific action, or where costs and expenses can be reduced through enactment of controls.

4. *There are no idle rumors in the market.* The market lives on rumors. So even if you perform a very in-depth analysis and you believe that you have considered all of the facts, you still need to recognize that the market actually decides on the basis of the latest rumor. And there are no idle rumors on Wall Street. All are given equal weight and will be reflected in sentiment. That includes all rumors—true ones, false ones, and even outrageous ones.

Recognize that no matter how carefully you study technical indicators, and no matter how thoroughly you analyze the significance of a matter, the smallest rumor can throw your stock's price in the opposite direction at any time. Remember that securities analysis is one tool that

KEY POINT

The idea of true or false does not matter when it comes to rumors in the market. Rumors affect prices; that is just the way it is.

helps you to gain a temporary edge over the market as a whole, but will not serve to guarantee profits under any circumstances.

5. *The stock market does not behave in a rational manner.* Not only does the market as a whole believe all rumors that are "out there," but it acts in an overall irrational manner to all news. For example, if a corporation's net profits are estimated at 9 percent, and they come in at 8.5 percent, the stock is likely to fall—solely because the outcome fell short of an expectation that might represent one analyst's opinion and nothing more. To the corporation and its board of directors, officers, and stockholders, the 8.5 percent return might represent a brilliant, dazzling result—but the stock will still fall.

There is nothing rational about the stock market, a fact that should be recognized as a basic rule for any study in this (and any other) cyclical market. In fact, the mere recognition of the market's irrationality is in itself an advantage. By being able to recognize when price movement makes no sense, you gain an advantage over the majority—that is, assuming that you do not fall prey to the "herd mentality" that characterizes

KEY POINT

Rational forces might exist in the stock market, but they have little or nothing to do with short-term price movement.

the majority of individuals in the market, not to mention the majority of institutional managers.

6. *The differences between fundamental analysis and technical analysis are important when studying cycles— it is all in the point of view.* Some investors shrug off the differences between the fundamental (financial results) and the technical (price movement), considering each to be just one aspect of the same process. They are not. Many people have learned that the best way to approach the question of securities analysis is to use some fundamental and some technical information, because both sides have important arguments and can provide valuable information. But the approach is different from each side. The fundamental analyst believes that the answers are to be found strictly in the dollars and cents of the market, and that it is the long-term value of a company that determines whether an investment is worthwhile. The technical analyst believes that price movement is determined not by the numbers, but by the market's perception of future value, and that being aware of how this process works makes the technician more astute.

Both sides are right, to a degree. It is the combination of fundamental and technical analysis that enables you to judge the market completely, for a very good reason: The market does consist of companies whose financial strength matters, but it also consists of an auction, and that auction and its participants have the final say on the question of price and value. Use both the fundamental and the technical sides to enhance your understanding of the market and of how the supply and demand cycle works.

KEY POINT

There are no direct conflicts between fundamental and technical schools, only a different point of view. The company's financial results and current market price of its stock are entirely unrelated.

7. *Cycles are affected by many factors outside of the market.* Another mistake common to investors is to forget that the market is not an isolated campus, where outside influences play no role. The importance of outside factors—politics, wars, world events, decisions by the Federal Reserve Board of Governors, the rate of inflation, individual senti-ment—all of these elements affect the market and the prices of stocks.

Look beyond the market itself, beyond the fundamental and technical information that is too widely available. Read world news and pay attention to outside economic developments, to politics at home and overseas, and to the mood that people demonstrate. Remember that markets tend to rise when people feel safe and secure and when there is little serious trouble; they tend to fall when people feel unsafe and insecure and when there is much unrest in the world.

KEY POINT

The market price of a stock does not change only because of what is going on in the market, a fact easily for-gotten if your entire world exists on Wall Street.

8. *Overreaction characterizes the market and affects the cycle.* In watching the way that the market reacts—that is to say, watching the collective daily price movements and levels of volume—we do not have a dependable or scien-tific indicator. The market is characterized by overreaction and by reaction that often is entirely out of proportion to the news or event. For example, a stock's value might fall in the light of a stunning year merely because an analyst predicted even better results, or because a competitor to that company announced expectations that the entire

industry would have a poor year, or because of some factor unrelated to the price of the stock.

When overreaction occurs over a period of time, it becomes a trend in and of itself. And to the degree that this continues, it also might affect the otherwise rational cycle of the market. Of course, the market does establish its own cycles by the changes and movements it experiences, but the irrationality of the market also defines it.

KEY POINT

Invariably, news or rumor creates too much response in the market. If you recognize this, you can do well in timing investment decisions based on short-term price reactions.

9. *You need to understand whether you are studying short-term price movement or long-term profit potential.* We mentioned before that it is important to be aware of the differences between fundamental and technical analysis. It also is important to be aware of which indicators are related to the short term, namely those related to immediate price movement and similar concerns, and which indicators tell you more about long-term prospects for growth.

Terms like *income* and *growth* are used rather freely to describe the differences between mutual funds within a family of funds, or to describe investment goals. But they have significant meaning, and for individual investors it becomes important to know whether to respond to immediate price concerns or take steps to build future potential. The more immediate is far more interesting because whether you are right or wrong, you will see results immediately. But in many respects, long-term growth potential will be more profitable and more satisfying in financial

> **KEY POINT**
>
> Be careful. If you are interested in long-term growth, do not be tricked into reacting to short-term indicators—that is the oldest mistake you can make.

terms. Neither approach is correct or incorrect, they are merely different.

10. *Nothing comes out the way we expect, especially in the market.* Prediction would be an uninteresting activity if outcomes were truly predictable. It is satisfying only because to be right means to guess, perceive, assume, or calculate something that no one knows, at least not in absolute terms. When predicting the future, you will be wrong more than right, because the future rarely comes out as we expect. And it is not just a matter of being right or wrong. In the future, the actual outcome is the only right answer; in addition, there is an infinite number of wrong answers as well.

   In the market, predicting is just as interesting and just as difficult as elsewhere. Even so, predicting is the great hobby and activity within the market. Everyone has much to say about what will happen in the near-term future, and greater attention is paid to predictions and their affect on stock prices than to whether anyone is actually making money. This is perhaps one of the more amazing aspects of the market. It might prove more valuable, whether in the short-term or long-term strategies of analysis, to attempt to predict supply and demand than to try to predict changes in stock prices. Supply and demand is more predictable than prices are, and might also show the way to more success in short-term investing. This is the topic of Chapter 2.

Predicting Supply and Demand

The whole point of trying to understand supply and demand is to improve your ability to beat the averages of the stock market. Most mutual fund managers (90 percent in the most recent year) do *not* beat the average. But what does that mean? Does it mean that mutual fund management is not doing a good job? Or does it mean that the funds represent such a large portion of the overall market that they cannot statistically be far from average?

The point is that the large impact of mutual funds on the market is not as readily understood as it might seem. It is disturbing at first glance that the vast majority perform under the market average. But then you also have to realize that mutual funds represent a huge portion of the total investment dollars in the market, so their impact might distort the apparent meaning of the outcome. Mutual funds also might affect supply and demand.

It is possible for a single group as large as the mutual funds to affect the outcomes of the market because such a large percentage of investment dollars is moved through those funds. In this regard, it is fair to say that mutual fund management collectively might affect supply and demand because, to a degree, they create it.

Unpredictability

To a large extent, supply and demand is as unpredictable as stock price movements themselves. Given some history, in a large overview supply and demand can be studied and its cause and effect recognized. But from day to day, this is not an easy task. Why does a stock's price rise and fall from one moment to another? In the confusion of the moment, it is not all that easy to predict how supply and demand operate. There are several reasons that supply and demand is unpredictable.

Market Forces Are Complex

The market itself is made up of an array of influences that, collectively, make any immediate analysis difficult. The financial press likes to simplify matters, reporting that the market rises or falls on "fears of interest rate changes" or "optimism concerning foreign markets." In reality, however, the forces of the market are too complex to analyze in a simple manner. The truth is that there are numerous forces at work, each affecting the market in subtle ways.

KEY POINT

News you hear "on the street" is oversimplified; in fact, many forces are at work creating and modifying supply and demand.

Market Forces Do Not Operate Logically

Even if we know the many forces affecting the market each day, we still cannot expect order or predictability—because the forces do not operate logically. Even if we could pin down the exact causes or combination of causes affecting stock prices, that would not mean that market reaction would be fair and reasonable. For example, if we could know that today's market will be pessimistic because of trouble in the Japanese financial markets, what does that mean? Will stock prices fall? By how much? Which issues will be the most affected? In actuality, prices might rise, some stocks will be affected and others will not, and the degree of rise or fall cannot be known in advance, even when the root causes are known. In short, no simplified causes for supply and demand changes (or the consequences to stock prices) are easily studied or anticipated.

KEY POINT

It is amazing that, while causes for price changes are invariably complex and involved, market experts have attempted consistently to simplify the reasons for those changes.

There Might Be More to the Story Than Just Market Forces

As we have seen time and again, the stock market is not a rational market that logically assesses information and then acts on it in a predictable manner. Besides the well-known market forces (economic news, political changes, and so forth), there are many intangible and even unnamed forces at work in the market, any of which might affect the supply and demand balance. Rumors about future market forces, by themselves, can cause significant upturns and downturns without any substance or even truth, creating the kind of chaos that characterizes short-term market changes. It is better to be aware of intermediate-term trends than to try to anticipate the supply and demand pattern on a daily basis. It simply cannot be done.

The ultimate point to be made about supply and demand and its cycles is that the entire matter is highly volatile and unpredictable.

> **KEY POINT**
>
> Causes beyond market forces can, and often do, have a lot to do with price changes. Supply and demand does not operate as clearly in the real world as it does in models.

This is the essence of market risk. No matter how much information you have available, and no matter how much analysis you perform, your timing might be unfortunate—and a stock you purchase might go down. By the same argument, the timing of selling cannot be a certain thing. A stock might rise dramatically moments after you sell. The reasons? They are complex, varied, and often entirely unrelated to anything going on in the market at the time.

> **KEY POINT**
>
> The unpredictability of supply and demand characterizes and defines market risk. You have no way to know with certainty when a decision is well-timed or ill-timed. This is what makes the stock market interesting.

Forms of Supply and Demand

Many people tend to think of supply and demand in only its most obvious form: The supply of stock compared to the demand for it. When demand increases, prices rise, and when demand falls (when there is more stock for sale than there are buyers interested in that stock), prices weaken and fall.

As true as these general rules of thumb are, there is more to supply and demand in the market. The astute technical investor needs to be aware of the subtleties in other matters concerning supply and demand.

First, companies make products and offer services. Supply and demand changes within industries as well as within companies. For example, an industry leader might be overtaken by a competitor, meaning that demand for the first company's products will begin tapering off over time. While such information is fundamental in character, the technical investor also needs to be aware of the likely future impact of such intraindustry changes.

Second, the supply of investors is not infinite. Be aware of the portion of the market represented by new investors and first-time investors, not to mention foreign investors. Also be aware of general trends in the population. Are today's trends going to be sustained indefinitely? Probably not. As the population average ages shift and as groups (like baby boom and baby bust populations) change, so do the trends in investment supply and demand.

Third, a company's stock cannot maintain a spectacular rise or fall in price indefinitely. Be aware of the tendency for matters to quiet down periodically. If a lot of investment volume and price change occurs, that does not mean the game has changed for a particular company's stock. It is more likely to signify that the level of activity is temporary and will taper off. That means that a trend toward ever-rising price levels will level off, or that a trend toward rapidly falling levels will cease. In many instances, the change surpasses a justified level so that a correction in price occurs in the opposite direction. This is the point at which many

KEY POINT

No trends move in the same direction forever. Always be looking out for the sudden reversal, because that is where your advantage often lies.

investors get in for the first time (usually at the top of the price trend), only to be surprised by a sudden correction in the opposite direction. The same might occur in a selling trend.

Fourth, the number of institutional investors (mutual funds, for example) might seem vast and infinite, but it is not. There is a limit to the number of funds that can form, attract investors, and then enter the market. Funds also are limited in terms of how much capital they can raise and spend. The market is finite and so is the amount of stock. An excess of investors buying through funds is not a positive sign—it is a sign of optimism that could well have the effect of driving up prices artificially, meaning a correction has to come at some point in the future, often the near future.

Fifth, there is a limit in the number of well-rated companies. Even the U.S. economy is finite, so that there is only so much prosperity to go around. Don't make the mistake of believing, even when times are exceedinly good, that the economy and the growth of prosperity is infinite and will go on forever. Optimism, as American as it is and as good as it feels, can deceive us and end up costing a lot of investment money.

Different Supply and Demand Markets

There are numerous forms of supply and demand and they exist in different markets or sectors of markets. For example, the well-known supply and demand for shares of stock is only a part of a larger machine, which is worldwide industry. The entire world of business is based on a larger version of supply and demand, and markets exist on many levels, including the following:

Products and Services

Every company listed in the exchanges offers some kind of product or service, sometimes both. No one company has complete control over its industry, so it must compete with other, similar companies, often better financed, better recognized by the public, and perhaps even better managed. This splits the demand for products and services among the competitors within each industry. If the number of companies offering products is too great, then the limited demand for those products will be spread thinly among them or, ultimately, some of the companies will go out of business or be forced to change with the times.

KEY POINT

There is only so much demand for products and services to go around. When supply exceeds the demand, something has to give—usually one of the companies in a particular industry.

Labor

Labor supply and demand is not as obvious as product supply and demand, but companies must compete to attract skilled, trained workers on all levels. If a company is unable to offer the combined salary and benefits package expected by workers—and offered by other companies—workers will not remain on the job and will take offers from other companies. When the demand for labor is high and the supply is relatively low, that drives up wages. The supply and demand market for labor varies as ceaselessly as the stock market (and most other supply and demand situations), because companies experience differing levels of work

KEY POINT

Labor, like other limited commodities, is subject to the rules of ever-changing supply and demand. When labor is plentiful, workers cannot easily negotiate for more money. When labor is scarce, it becomes more valuable.

and demand for their products. The company needs skilled, permanent workers and supervisors, but does not want to pay unnecessarily high wages and salaries; thus the variation.

Management

One of the fiercest markets is that for talented, capable top management. Big companies pay enormous salaries to chief executive officers (CEOs) and other high-level managers. To some, these salaries seem out of line. But in many instances, they are justified. Why? Because the individual receiving the salary is capable of increasing profits to such a level that her salary represents a bargain to the company. The organization does not want the talented leader to go elsewhere, so it offers an abundantly attractive salary and benefits package. In many respects, the CEO's job is to increase profits, but more to the point, the real job is to maintain the stock's market price.

KEY POINT

The chief executive officer often is paid to keep the stock price high because so many high-placed officers and board members have salaries *and* stock options.

Stock (Equity) Investment Sources

Companies need to pay for their continued growth and operation. This requires outside investment in the form of equity (stock). Stockholders own a piece of the company as a benefit of turning over their investment capital. Companies need the outside funds because they invest their day-to-day cash in accounts receivable, inventory, and other short-term assets, as well as spending it on capital equipment needed for sustained growth. So investors are important not only because they supply cash, but also because that cash is the company's lifeblood.

KEY POINT

Big companies cannot operate without investment capital, and stockholders supply those companies with the cash needed to fund accounts receivable, inventories, and other assets. Investors and their dollars are finite, just like stock prices.

Bond (Debt) Investment Sources

In addition to needing equity capital, companies also depend on debt investments. Individuals who purchase corporate bonds are debt investors. They provide capital to the company in exchange for payments of interest. The company needs to limit the amount of debt it acquires, because ever-growing interest payments erode profits and penalize stockholders. So the well-led corporation has to limit the ratio of debt to equity. Of course, there is only a limited number of debt investors, so the forces of supply and demand dictate how debt investments occur. When a lot of money is available, the company can lower its offered interest rate. But when money is scarce, the company has to raise its rates to compete with other corporations.

KEY POINT

A limited supply of debt investors raises interest rates, and an abundant supply has the opposite effect.

Analysts' Attention and Approval

Everyone involved with the market realizes that the opinions of analysts are all important. Those who are especially observant also see that opinions may be based on intelligent study of the company and its fundamentals—but that the outcome within the market often has little or nothing to do with profit and loss. It is a perception of future value that determines the stock's present value. Thus, companies hope that analysts will look favorably on them, but they also recognize that analysts have to consider everything in relative terms. Thus, a well-managed company might appear less than exciting next to a more promising competitor. With only so much "top approval" to go around, competition for analysts' opinions is fierce.

KEY POINT

The analyst has much to say about a company's stock value, but the analyst cannot give glowing approval to all companies because good and bad are value judgments made in comparison.

Institutional Investment Dollars

Finally, the market for institutional investment dollars is huge. Mutual funds, pension and profit sharing plans, insurance companies, and other institutions have a massive amount of equity to invest in the market. When a large mutual fund decides to take a sizable position in a company's stock, that is a significant form of approval. On the other hand, when an institution with large holdings decides to dump a company's stock,

KEY POINT

Institutional investment capital represents such a large portion of the market and its investment capital that the relative influence of the individual investor is negligible.

that is an important negative signal. Accordingly, the big institutional investors have a great deal of influence within the market. They can create supply and demand by their own decisions to buy, hold, or sell.

The Economic Cycle in the Stock Market

A lot is written about economic cycles, but the term has several different meanings. The *real* economic cycle refers to the overall U.S. economy and its relative health. That is not necessarily important to what is going on in the stock market.

The economic cycle does refer to the health of business, of course, but only insofar as the fundamentals apply. In other words, it is a value judgment concerning present and future profits, the financial strength of a company or industry, and the effect of economics (interest rates, unemployment, inflation, etc.) on future profitability. The economic cycle, then, is actually a very basic and broad fundamental indicator.

KEY POINT

The overall economic cycle affects the financial results of companies. It is a broad fundamental indicator.

The stock market, unlike the companies whose stocks are listed within it, does not always act according to the real economic cycle. It has a supply and demand cycle of its own. Although the economic cycle has a very important impact on profits of listed companies, the market itself acts and reacts to *perceptions* of future profitability. That could mean that economic news affects the market, perhaps even that markets will overreact to such news. It also could mean that the market's actions and responses to news are entirely independent of what is going on in the economic cycle.

Where does perception of future value come from? When viewing the market as a whole, it is probably impossible to see clearly what factors affect stock prices, either directly or indirectly. There are so many different things that add to market perception that we cannot know all of them. But some are worth noting.

The Stock Analyst

Among the sources adding to the perception of future value, the analyst plays an all important role. The analyst studies the fundamentals and forecasts the next quarter's sales and profits. This sets the standard. If a company's performance is better than the analyst's prediction, the stock's price usually goes up. If it is worse (even if results are spectacular), the stock's price usually falls. This, at any rate, is the general rule of thumb. This is true because the expectation of future profits is believed to be factored into the stock price. The belief that the current stock price reflects all known information is called the *efficient market theory*.

KEY POINT

The efficient market theorist believes that the current price of a stock is affected by all known information, including the analyst's predictions.

The Institutional Investor

Institutional investors such as mutual funds make a clear statement to other investors by the actions they take. When an institutional investor purchases a large block of stock, or when it sells a large block of stock, other investors may follow the cue. Even if they do not, the actions of large investors affect the market perception of future value—directly.

> ## KEY POINT
> Perceptions of future value are affected directly by the actions of institutional investors because their actions involve large blocks of stock.

Rumors and Information

As we have observed before, the market is fueled by rumors and speculation—about anything and everything. Unsubstantiated "news" filters constantly throughout companies, in lunchrooms and cocktail lounges, on the street, and by telephone. Those people who work in the market are unable to distinguish between true and false rumors because the flow of these rumors is constant.

> ## KEY POINT
> The market runs on rumors. Some are true and some are false, and it is impossible to tell them apart.

The Financial Press

Another segment of the market that cannot be ignored is the extensive financial press. This includes newspapers, magazines, television programs, and subscription services. It is possible to

> ## KEY POINT
> There is so much information about the market that one cannot know how much—if any—is reliable.

find information supporting any and all points of view, from the most serious and analytical to the downright bizarre. In such an environment, it is difficult to determine which—if any—information is reliable.

Economists

There are many economists in the world, and they are notorious for having strong opinions *and* for rarely being right. George Bernard Shaw is believed to have said: "If all of the economists in the world were laid end to end, they wouldn't reach a conclusion."

KEY POINT

Economists, like so many experts, have only opinions about the future, and no actual knowledge. Sometimes, even an educated guess is of little real value.

Individual People

The ultimate judge of the market and of the potential for future value is the individual. The people who make up the investing public, whether directly or through mutual funds and other institutional structures, not only have the last word, but have much to say about whether their perceptions come true. After all, the primary reason that a company earns profits is the trust of its customers and investors.

KEY POINT

The individual investor determines the future of the stock market by where he places money—and trust.

Variation between a Company's Cycle and Its Stock's Cycle

Any observer of the market will be struck by an enigma: A company experiences a specific economic cycle of its own, but its stock doesn't necessarily follow suit. This is one of the dilemmas of the market: It is truly difficult to know with certainty how and when a stock's price will change.

Companies have very specific business cycles tied to the seasons and to the economy. For example, construction companies are active during the warmer months and relatively inactive when the weather is poor. Public utility companies experience a business cycle tied to interest rates because they carry a lot of debt. Thus, higher interest rates adversely affect their profits. Every industry has its own peculiar traits that determine its business cycle.

Given that, one would think that a stock's price would follow or at least approximate the business cycle of the company. But that is not the case. Why is the company's business cycle—its own personalized economic cycle, if you will—so specific, and yet its own stock so unpredictable? One answer is that investors accept the business cycle as one of the risks in investing in a particular company, and because this is factored into the stock's price at any given time, it does not affect the investor's perception. In other words, the problems related to business cycles already are reflected in the stock's price (the efficient market theory at work), so trying to anticipate changes in stock prices by considering business cycles is a mistake.

KEY POINT

There is no direct relationship between business cycles and stock prices. There should be. But then again, maybe there should not.

Imagine what it would be like if all investors knew in advance that a stock's market value would rise or fall because a predictable change in the company's business cycle was about to occur. In such a world, a financial analyst might say, "It will rain next week, so construction company stocks will lose 5 percent of their value," or "The weather will be beautiful this month, so construction company stocks will rise."

Most people recognize at once the futility of such speculation. Having such knowledge in advance would, by its nature, defeat the idea of predictability. If everyone had the same information and interpreted it the same way, then there would be no risk in the market. And no adventure. Another point to remember: The complete absence of risk also means the complete absence of reward; that is, profit.

KEY POINT

If you could know in advance how a stock's price was going to change, so would everyone else. And without risk, there also can be no profit.

Watching Stock Prices Over Time

The tendency for well-managed companies to see growth in their stock's value over time is well documented. For many investors, however, this is not a very interesting phenomenon. Some people are interested in shorter-term profits, in finding the new spectacular initial public offering, or in turning a fast profit. Speculators are not necessarily wrong about their approach to the market; they just don't want to wait out a long-term growth cycle. And because they take bigger risks than long-term investors, speculators are wrong much of the time; they often lose more money than they would like because they are risk takers.

KEY POINT

Speculators are not always wrong; they are just wrong more often than they would like.

It is a mistake to overlook the direct and inescapable relationship between risk and profit. Risk varies because the potential for profit—or loss—varies as well. The greater the risk of loss, the greater the potential reward. And the lower the risk, the lower the potential reward in the form of profits.

If you watch a stock's price over time, you will realize that the short-term variations of several dollars per share are meaningless, in one respect. As you observe the decade-long growth of a company's stock value, it may be apparent that the growth was steady and predictable based on consistent profits, dividend payments, and sales growth. Even so, the momentary changes in the stock's price might have appeared volatile at times, moving upward and downward in seemingly random fashion from day to day.

KEY POINT

A stock's short-term fluctuations are not as important to long-term growth as the consistency of matters such as sales, profits, and dividend payments over many years.

Each investor needs to decide whether to invest for the long term or to "play the market" by trying to guess when waves of stock movement are cresting or crashing. These are different approaches. The short-term investor might depend more on technical indicators, whereas the longer-term investor tends to

KEY POINT

You can act as a fundamentalist or as a technician or as both. The decision is an individual one. Long-term growth is predictable, though not very interesting. And short-term speculation has potential for higher profits (or losses), and is much more interesting.

watch the fundamentals. This does not exclude either from paying attention to both forms of analysis. It also does not mean you should not adopt both strategies. Why not put some portion of your portfolio into blue chip stocks whose long-term growth prospects are excellent—perhaps even certain—but not terribly interesting, and use another portion of your capital for speculation?

As you devise your own individual strategy, the question of risk and reward should be on your mind. Recognize that the potential for making a lot of money in a few days is accompanied by an unavoidably higher risk. Perhaps the efficient market theory should state this with some certainty. Thus, we will invent our own market efficiency rule: The market doles out rewards and punishments with equal severity, but with extraordinary unpredictability.

The Key to Prediction of Future Price Movement

If you desire a view into the future, look to the past.

This advice, of course, is easily given but more difficult to take. The past might be a useful indicator, but it really doesn't tell you what will happen in the future. It is likely that too many factors have changed: economic cause and effect, nature of the competition, management of the company, mood in the market, and timing. Industries and companies grow and fade in popularity for reasons beyond any analytical sense, so you cannot use the past to predict the future with certainty.

What, then, can you use to predict future price movement? The truth is, there are no certain methods for such a task. You need to combine all of the analytical tools useful in the stock of companies to determine what *might* influence future price movement. The truth is, you cannot predict with accuracy; you only can make an informed estimate. By doing this correctly, you can hope

KEY POINT

You cannot accurately predict the future. But you can arm yourself with a range of sensible analyses and beat the averages. In the market *that* spells success.

to beat the averages, but you can never depend on your estimates being right all of the time.

It is a mistake to aim for certainty at all times. You never can be certain about what is going to occur, and you cannot be accurate all of the time. It is this uncertain nature of the market that is both intriguing and disturbing—depending on whether your estimates lead to profits or mislead you into losses. At best, you can expect a mix of the two.

The trick is in determining which indicators to follow, which devices to use in your arsenal. Which ones work? Do today's popular tools provide useful information tomorrow? Do you need to modify your mix of analysis constantly? These are questions you need to answer for yourself. Don't ignore any fundamental or technical indicator that might add to your knowledge about how prices change or why, and never settle into a routine that will ignore potentially more valuable indicators in the future. In coming chapters, some of the technical indicators and approaches to analysis will be explained in detail and with examples. For now, consider this basic rule of thumb:

The analysis you employ in the study of stock prices needs to encompass enough variables so that your risk of being taken by surprise is minimized.

This single rule of thumb might be the best one to remember, because in the market everything changes quickly. So rather than adopt an approach involving a limited number of tests, you need to always keep your eyes open for the potential of an unexpected surprise. Think about the important and dramatic market events you have observed. None were expected. None were apparent to analysts in advance, and few, if any, were forecast reliably by the experts. The market takes everyone by surprise, because it is wild and unpredictable. It also is random.

KEY POINT

No important change in the market is predicted with consistency. Analysis cannot warn you in advance of the unexpected; it only can prepare you and protect you from being caught completely unprepared. It is the nature of risk to surprise the investor.

Overcoming the Random Nature of the Market

Because the nature of the market is random and haphazard, it is full of risk. Some analysts will argue this point, claiming that the market is highly predictable. Technicians especially will point to charts as proof that price movement is always predictable if you know how to read the patterns. The flaw in this argument is that patterns, like every other element of analysis, have more than one possible meaning. It also is highly suspect to believe that a visual trading pattern in the past is absolutely revealing about the future. Charting offers you some valuable analytical tools, but it does not predict the future with certainty.

The future in all respects is random and cannot be known. The purpose of analysis should be to minimize your exposure to

KEY POINT

A study of the past always shows the rules that were followed. But in the future, all of the rules will have been changed—and no one knows what they will be.

unexpected risk. It is not—as some would claim—intended to work as a tool that promotes your ability to forecast accurately most of the time. In the market, a constant game is being played. The objective is to be right more often than the other investors or analysts. Even in those financial programs that consider themselves to be seriously dedicated to the fundamentals (like *Wall Street Week*), the real interest in the show invariably comes down to predictions about future price movement, study of the Dow Jones Industrial Average (DJIA) (as arbitrary and nonfundamental as you can get), and a straight-faced series of predictions about where the market is going. So although the experts you see on television and read in the financial press claim to be dedicated fundamentalists, they really are in the prediction game—as is most of Wall Street.

How do you overcome the random nature of the market? By not playing the prediction guessing game. Abandon that and devote yourself to a serious study of the market. Select intelligent indicators, technical or fundamental, that help you to achieve your real purpose—not to predict the future accurately, but to anticipate likely outcomes and to arrange your investments to minimize the risk of loss. In doing this, you also increase your opportunity for profits. This is how successful investors proceed: not preoccupied with being right more than someone else in guessing the future, but knowing when they are overexposed to the risk of loss.

Example: One investor uses analysis to estimate when the stocks in his portfolio have risen to an assumed high. At such times, he sells the stock and moves those funds to other issues he has been watching, or parks funds temporarily in a money market fund. He is sometimes wrong. Markets continue to rise, sometimes to spectacular heights, and he misses the opportunity to make a higher profit. But more often, his indicators are correct and his timing is wise. He often repurchases the same stock after a correction has occurred. On average, this investor avoids loss, reduces his exposure to risk, and makes a profit in his portfolio.

In this example, the investor moved funds out of a stock after a predetermined level of growth was achieved. This is done because a goal is met. It helps avoid the problem seen all too often in the market. An investor buys stock and it goes up in value. Then it goes back down, and an opportunity to take profits has been lost. In such a situation, investors often beat themselves up with the "should have" thinking that often characterizes the market. But remember, the purpose of analysis is not to avoid risk. It is to reduce your exposure to the unexpected changes in the market—corrections, for example.

The market is random and that cannot be avoided. All you can do is to help yourself avoid exposure beyond what you can afford. Your analysis should be based on sensibly established investing goals and standards. In addition, you need to recognize that as far as you are concerned, the market as represented by the DJIA often has little or nothing to do with the stocks in which you have invested. Adopt the policy that for you the market represents those stocks you own or are thinking of owning in the future. The Dow is an interesting but limited index and, in the long run, it tells you nothing beyond the mood of the market—and that mood is wrong as often as it is right.

CHAPTER 3

The Dow Theory and How It Works

Everyone would like to have a dependable theory about the market. How it works, why prices change, and when changes will occur and by how much. As we saw in Chapter 2, the nature of the market is to be unpredictable.

The *Dow Theory* serves as one of the basic models to explain market movement. Charles H. Dow and Edward C. Jones (better known as "Dow Jones") developed several ideas about 100 years ago to try to identify the primary causes of market change. With all of the ideas that have come and gone since, the Dow-Jones work remains a cornerstone of opinion within the market and probably will remain so for many years to come.

Dow came up with the idea of tracking overall market change with the use of an index. He believed that trends in the market could be used to anticipate and explain movements in stocks generally (and, one would hope, within individual issues as well). Dow's background in Wall Street matters was extensive. He was a partner in a Wall Street New York Stock Exchange (NYSE) member firm for six years before meeting Edward C. Jones. The two formed Dow, Jones & Company, Inc., and the first edition of their new financial newspaper, *The Wall Street Journal*, was published on July 8, 1889.*

The Dow Theory was not a direct invention of Dow's, although it is loosely based on some essays he published before his death in 1902. The Dow Theory was developed by a friend of Dow's, Samuel Nelson. In his book *The ABCs of Stock Speculation* Nelson laid out the principles of Dow's philosophy. Dow's successor as editor of *The Wall Street Journal*, William Peter Hamilton, further developed the Dow Theory. His predictions about changes in the market became a regular and popular feature of the paper, and he also published *The Stock Market Barometer* (1926), in which he further developed the ideas that came to be known as the Dow Theory.

Ironically, the basis for all of this theorizing was rooted in Dow's original observations about the cyclical nature of trading. Dow did not mean to have his ideas serve as the basis for the market, but rather as a guide for business. This is the core of the Dow Theory. Dow observed that when the market as a whole was on the move, either upward or downward, stocks tended to act in concert, moving in generally the same direction. In other words, there is a tendency for many stocks to be followers of the lead established by a few large market leaders. This is true in business just as it is in the market, and Dow believed that his discovery of this tendency could be used to help businesses make forecasts of cyclical change.

To make his point, Dow identified 12 stocks[†] he considered to be market leaders, on the theory that those stocks would indicate the general mood of the market. As they rose, so would the market as a whole, and vice versa. In 1916, the list grew to 20

---

*The publication was originally called the *Customer's Afternoon Letter* and began publication in 1882.

[†]The original 12 stocks were American Cotton Oil; American Sugar; American Tobacco; Chicago Gas; Distilling & Cattle Feeding; General Electric; Leclede Gas; National Lead; North American; Tennessee Coal & Iron; U.S. Leather Preferred; and U.S. Rubber.

stocks, and in 1928, it was expanded again to its current level of 30.*

As of February, 1999, the 30 stocks in the Dow Jones Industrial Average (DJIA) are:

Symbol	Name
ALD	AlliedSignal Inc.
AA	Aluminum Company of America (Alcoa)
AXP	American Express Co.
T	AT&T Corp.
BA	Boeing Co.
CAT	Caterpillar Inc.
CHV	Chevron Corp.
C	Citigroup Inc.
KO	Coca-Cola Co.
DD	DuPont Co.
EK	Eastman Kodak Co.
XON	Exxon Corp.
GE	General Electric Corp.
GM	General Motors Corp.
GT	Goodyear Tire & Rubber Co.
HWP	Hewlett-Packard Co.
IBM	International Business Machines Corp.
IP	International Paper Co.
JPM	J.P. Morgan & Co.
JNJ	Johnson & Johnson
MCD	McDonald's Corp.
MRK	Merck & Co.
MMM	Minnesota Mining & Manufacturing Co.
MO	Philip Morris Cos.
PG	Proctor & Gamble Co.
S	Sears, Roebuck & Co.
UK	Union Carbide Corp.

---

*For more information about the Dow Jones Industrial Average, check the Dow Jones Web site, www.averages.dowjones.com.

Symbol	Name
UTX	United Technologies Corp.
WMT	Wal-Mart Stores Inc.
DIS	Walt Disney Co.

These 30 stocks collectively account for about one-fifth of all the value in the American market, which is worth more than $8 trillion, and about one-fourth of the value on the NYSE.*

The Dow Theory Explained

When Dow developed his ideas, and when those ideas were later expanded into the formal representations of the market as used today, it was all about the analysis of *trends*. After all, the index is supposed to represent the leading issues in the market, thus setting trends for the rest of the market to follow. The Dow Theory contains the following essential tenets.

The Market Demonstrates Three Distinct Trends

Dow concluded from his observations about the tendency of stocks to move together that bull or bear markets were predictable. If successive advances exceed previous high levels *and* declines stop before falling below previous low levels, then a bull market is underway—so states the Dow Theory. By the same argument, when previous low levels are exceeded on the down side *and* the market fails to rise above prior high levels, then a bear market has begun. So in short, an upward trend is not an isolated event, but rather a series of highs that exceed previous high levels, and a downward trend is the establishment of lower lows than before.

Trend analysis forms the basis for definition of new trends, whether bull or bear in nature. As with all cycles, it is impossible to establish new changes in the market without confirmation

---

*Source: Dow Jones & Co. Web site, www.averages.dowjones.com/abtdjia.html, as of February 17, 1999.

by way of subsequent events, that is, higher highs or lower lows.

Adding to the trend analysis in the market, William Hamilton wrote about the three movements observed in the market:

> There are three movements in the market which are in progress at one and the same time. These are, first, the day-to-day movement resulting mainly from the operation of the traders, which may be called the tertiary movement; second, the movement usually extending from 20 to 60 days, reflecting the ebb and flow of speculative sentiment which is called the secondary movement; and, third, the main movement, usually extending for a period of years, caused by the adjustment of prices to underlying values, usually called the primary movement.[*]

The identification of three movements leads to further definition of the types of markets that are experienced at a given point in the cycle, and how they are characterized. A *primary bull market* is a long-term trend toward ever-increasing prices, interrupted by corrections as investors take profits. In a bull market, even severe bad news may be discounted so that such news has minimal effect on prices. The enthusiasm and optimism of investors during bull markets is always recognized in hindsight, but it is difficult to see in the midst of such times. A *primary bear market* is characterized by long-term overall price declines. Such a market will experience significant rallies—upswings in price—because bear markets constantly present bargains from momentary overreaction in terms of price decline.

KEY POINT

As with all trends, it is not an isolated incident, but a specific series of incidents, that establishes a new direction.

---

[*]*The Wall Street Journal*, September 17, 1904.

Everything Is Discounted because of the Averages

This tenet is a bit more straightforward and less complex. The hypothesis is that the closing prices of stocks—collectively—reflect all that is known or believed at that time. This would include information about the company, the economy, and the market—everything that affects supply and demand. Of course, this is only a theory, and it assumes not only that the market is efficient, but also that investors are efficient in gathering information. As we said, it is only a theory.

KEY POINT

To better explain how the market works, the Dow Theory presents several beliefs—and that is all they are—that add to an understanding of market forces, but are not hard-and-fast rules of investing.

Trends Are Definitely Established When Three Events Occur

One of the principles of trend analysis is that a real trend has to be recognized by some specific measurement. We cannot simply look at a momentary event in isolation and call it a trend. Under the Dow Theory, three events have to occur before a trend is established. In a bull market, the three events are:

1. Well-informed investors purchase stock in slow times when prices are low and the market mood is negative or apathetic. These investors anticipate future change.
2. Earnings increase in the underlying company, leading to further interest and investment in its stock.
3. A company comes into favor with the market as a whole, and everyone buys its stock. This, of course, creates more demand and drives up the price further. In other words, the

technical indicator (popularity) follows the fundamental indicator (higher profits).

In a bear market, the three events are:

1. Well-informed investors recognize that a stock's price has risen in step with growth in earnings. Because they know the company will not be able to maintain such high earnings levels, these investors sell their stock.
2. It becomes increasingly difficult to find willing buyers, so the lack of demand leads to a decline in the stock's price.
3. The market as a whole sees the decline in price and rushes to sell shares. This further erodes the stock's value.

As you might recognize, the three-part process is nothing more than a formalized observation about the forces of supply and demand. It is invariably a minority of keen, analytical, and far-sighted investors who see the coming changes in advance of the market as a whole, and who lead the market into primary trends.

KEY POINT

One of the strengths of the Dow Theory is its recognition that changes in the market happen in stages; that a minority of investors lead the market; and, most of all, that the majority usually do not see the change coming until after it has occurred.

Trends Are Determined by Stock Prices

Many analysts consider factors beyond just the price, but under the Dow Theory the price is the determining factor in the establishment or identification of a trend. This is where trading patterns become important.

As rallies go through previously set highs twice in a row, that is called a bullish indication. In other words, it is not enough that a previous level is exceeded once; the trend is confirmed only when succeeding rallies both break the previously set record. The same is true for bearish trends on the downside.

The relationship between price and volume is of further help in confirming the trend. As a general rule, volume tends to increase when prices rise, and to decrease as prices fall. So when this tendency is not present, it is believed that the prevailing trend might be on the verge of reversal.

KEY POINT

Under the Dow Theory, closing prices are the only prices considered even though a range of different prices might be experienced during a single trading day.

Two Averages Must Confirm to Establish a Trend

The Dow Jones Industrial Average and the Dow Jones Transportation Average have to be considered together when determining whether a trend has been established. This is one of the tenets, or rules, of the Dow Theory.

A bull trend is signaled only when both averages rise above their previous highs; a bear trend is signaled only when both averages fall below their previous lows. The production of goods and the transportation of goods is directly related; however, this also assumes that price movement in the market follows the economic condition (fundamentals) of listed companies. This is not necessarily the case. The need for both averages to confirm one another is only another device to prove that a trend is being established. While the economic condition of underlying companies is important in the long term, it cannot dependably be believed to reflect such matters as promptly as a trend is established.

If only one of the averages breaks through previous highs in successive rallies (or falls below previous lows in successive

> ### KEY POINT
>
> A trend is not a trend until it is signaled in two averages—industrial and transportation—which confirm the new direction.

declines), that does not establish a trend. The trend is confirmed only when both the industrial and transportation averages meet these criteria.

The Trend Stays in Effect until Both Averages Reverse

Just as confirmation of a new trend is required to establish the trend, the Dow Theory states that the trend remains in effect until both the industrial and transportation averages show a reversal.

> ### KEY POINT
>
> It is difficult to recognize new trends when they begin *and* when they end. The Dow Theory requires identification of both by the same rules. Remember, the Dow Theory's purpose is to identify reversals of primary trends.

The Random Walk Hypothesis

One market theory, the *Random Walk Hypothesis,* holds that all price movement is the result of supply and demand in varying degrees of knowledge (some well-informed and some badly informed), and that as a consequence, all price change is random. There are several points that have to be made regarding this idea.

First, an objective study of any hypothesis requires objective analysis by those who are interested. In other words, the testing of a hypothesis requires application of the scientific method.* This means that the individual considering the Random Walk Hypothesis would have to begin with an open mind. In the stock market, large numbers of analysts, managers, brokers, experts, and specialists are paid for their insight and knowledge. They cannot be objective.

KEY POINT

If the Random Walk Hypothesis is correct, then an entire industry of experts is being paid for knowing something that they cannot know. This is a troubling idea to the experts.

So we have a poor starting point. Anyone who is paid to tell you about how to invest—including, perhaps, financial authors—might have a bias against the Random Walk Hypothesis because, by accepting it, one has to accept the idea that it does not matter where you invest your money. If it is all random, no degree of knowledge can possibly improve your odds.

A second factor getting in the way of an objective study of this hypothesis is the tendency for investors to want some certainty. Ignoring for a moment the possibility that the Random Walk Hypothesis might be true, consider this: Investors want to believe that it is possible to forecast with some degree of certainty what will happen under a given set of circumstances. A well-managed

---

*The scientific method attempts to objectively analyze a matter, with an equal interest in proving or disproving a hypothesis. In order to prove absolutely that something is so, it also is necessary to eliminate all of the alternate hypotheses. In matters of theory, this cannot be done, but using the scientific method as an approach to determining validity is a good start.

company that earns high profits and pays out dividends, outper-
forms its competition, has a superb management team, and constantly expands its markets and improves on its products and
services—all of these things together—should translate to growth
in the value of stock. And historically, this has been the case.
Investors want to believe that if they select companies with the
characteristics that have led to long-term growth in the past, they
improve their chances of benefiting from the same thing occurring in the future. The Random Walk Hypothesis disputes this
idea, stating that it doesn't matter where you invest, because all
price movement is arbitrary.

KEY POINT

It is difficult to seriously consider any hypothesis that would invade our belief systems, whether true or
false.

In spite of the biases that anyone interested in investing holds,
the facts speak for themselves. Companies whose stock rises over
many decades also tend to be well-managed, earning consistent
profits and paying out dividends. There is nothing random about
that. You might consider the source of a bias for or against the
Random Walk Hypothesis. But in the final analysis, you should
consider the facts. What are the characteristics of well-managed
companies? And how do those characteristics affect stock prices?
Historically, better-managed companies earn profits and their
stocks rise as a result. Thus, the Random Walk Hypothesis just
doesn't hold up in a study of historical earnings. And poorly
managed companies eventually are overrun by competition and
absorbed or forced out of business. This is seen again and again.
Still, the Random Walk Hypothesis is intriguing. It is supported
by some in the academic community, where professors enjoy
ideas but might have little or no practical real-world experience,

KEY POINT

Most proponents of the Random Walk Hypothesis promote the idea but do not really know how the real world works. Anyone who studies supply and demand knows that smart management leads to profits, and that profits lead to growth in capital.

and as you might imagine, it has never become a popular theory on Wall Street.

The Random Walk Hypothesis is in some respects the antithesis of the Dow Theory. It takes the extreme view that you cannot predict the market because the force of supply and demand is unpredictable, random, and arbitrary. Such theories can be helpful, though, balancing our point of view about the market. The Dow Theory aims for an elegant solution, a pure understanding of the predictability of change based on the study of trends in the market. Perhaps the idea that foresight can be as dependable as hindsight is too ideal, just as the Random Walk Hypothesis is too limiting. By studying the Random Walk Hypothesis, you develop a more thorough appreciation of the Dow Theory, and perhaps a balanced point of view about both.

Theories and Practical Application

Theories are of little value unless they help us to perform tasks in the real world—the world where application is required. Investing is such a world, you need to decide whether to buy, sell, hold, or simply stay out of the market.

The Dow Theory does have practical applications. It has been developed and studied over the past century, and there is much to be said for its tenets. The Dow Theory remains "just a theory" because it does not provide evidence that it is correct and it cannot be used consistently to always know which direction the market will move. Even if you can know, you cannot always time it precisely. And like all cycles, the supply and demand cycle of the market is characterized by misleading interim movements opposite of the larger trend. Telling the difference between the trend and those countermovements is no easy matter.

KEY POINT

The Dow Theory is useful for the big picture of the market, but it cannot tell us how to act on a day-to-day basis.

On a practical level, the Dow Theory, like the averages on which its tenets are based, provides a useful barometer that can be used as one of several forecasting tools. It may confirm your suspicions or provide you with information at variance with other sources. In either case, it is intelligence. And in the market, intelligence gathering is all important. Even rumors are a form of intelligence, and the market gobbles up every juicy tidbit that is out there. In the case of the Dow Theory, real value is not in the form of rumor, but in the form of speculation about the likely significance of the current model. In other words, the Dow Theory is the best form of trend analysis *based on stock prices* that is available. Other forms of trend analysis meant to study fundamentals—like sales and profits, for example—provide different types of information. If your interest is in tracking price movement and trying to place some definition on likely future change, the Dow Theory is the best tool available.

The Random Walk Hypothesis cannot be dismissed without at least granting that there is something to the idea. After all, when you consider the vast number of variables affecting price, including some that reflect no discernible reason whatsoever, it is possible that, to a degree, short-term price movements are random.

KEY POINT

Because both the Dow Theory and the Random Walk Hypothesis reject short-term price movement as having any value, we might as well assume that short-term movement should be ignored.

Remember, though, that even the Dow Theory grants that short-term (first phase) movement largely should be ignored.

If you consider these two approaches to be exact opposites in terms of theory, then any points on which they agree have some validity. Thus, short-term fluctuations in stock prices probably reflect the reactions, overreactions, and illogical supply and demand factors in the immediate—the relatively chaotic changes that cannot be pinned down because they have no actual cause.

With this in mind, we might consider that the Random Walk Hypothesis has more validity than proponents of the Dow Theory admit, at least to some degree. So we might value both theories by arriving at two of our own general rules:

1. The Dow Theory gains greater validity with more time under study. Because it is a pure form of trend analysis, the larger sample provides greater accuracy. (This conforms to one of the tenets of the Dow Theory, that the averages discount everything.)
2. The Random Walk Hypothesis is entirely right when applied to short-term price movement. However, the greater the time involved, the less valid this hypothesis becomes.

Understanding Market Risk

The value in understanding theories and hypotheses about price movement is in how they help you to better perceive what is going on in the market. You need to know what elements create or cause

> ## KEY POINT
>
> Risk and opportunity are inseparable elements of the market. They move and change in direct relation to one another.

risk, how that risk affects or endangers your portfolio, and, even more to the point, how the related opportunity might increase your profits.

The term *risk* is used loosely in discussions of the stock market, too often without a real understanding what it means. As an investor, you are exposed to several forms of risk. The best-known of these is *market risk*, which includes a range of risks related to losses and price fluctuations. Market risk should be studied in more detail because it involves more than the obvious price movement risk. Market risk has numerous subforms including price risk, opportunity risk, diversification risk, liquidity risk, and inflation risk.

Price Risk

The most apparent form of risk is the risk that the market price of your stock will drop. But even this well-known risk is more complex than that. For example, one form of price risk involves holding stock that should be sold. A hold decision exposes you to the risk that prices will drop.

There is a corresponding opportunity in the equation, which is called *price opportunity*. A decision to sell exposes you to the opportunity to take your profits or cut losses, but it also takes away the potential to benefit from price increase. A decision to hold continues the price opportunity. You have price opportunity available only if you are in the market and at risk, meaning that you can only profit if you also expose yourself to loss. As with all forms of investing, staying out of the market helps you avoid all forms of market risk, but it also deprives you of all forms of price opportunity.

Opportunity Risk

Another form of risk, not to be confused with the previous discussion of price risk and opportunity, is what is called opportunity risk. As long as your capital is invested in one choice or series of choices, it is not available to invest in other stocks or non-stock investments. Thus, you stand to lose the opportunity to profit if and when those investments' value rises.

The corresponding part of this equation is the potential for gain that you have by deciding on one stock over another. This is a choice among many opportunities, so a form of risk is based on the question of which opportunity is best to take.

Diversification Risk

Diversification is the spreading of risk among several dissimilar investments. It is the problem of diversification risk that leads many investors to mutual funds. In a fund, you have thorough diversification even if your capital is limited. It is important to invest your money in enough different ways so that any single tendency does not threaten your entire portfolio. To some, this means buying different stocks. To others, it means buying stocks in different industries. And to still others, it means investing only a portion of the total portfolio in the market.

There also is diversification opportunity. In one form, not diversifying provides you with an opportunity. If you invest all of your money in one stock and it rises dramatically, then you earn a profit. Through diversification, profits might be offset by losses elsewhere. But this gets down to the essence of diversification: Just as profits might be offset by losses, so losses are offset by profits.

Liquidity Risk

Every investor has to face the problem of needing a ready reserve of cash—liquidity. If all of your money is tied up in stocks that you don't want to sell, you have no ready reserve. You should set aside some cash for emergencies or, at the very least, have a line of credit that you can access for unexpected problems, such as automobiles breaking down, repairs to the house, disasters like fires or floods, and so forth.

A liquidity opportunity also exists. Remember that cash sitting idle is losing money because it is not at work. So having your capital fully invested provides you with a form of benefit that you lose by setting up a cash reserve. Today's institutions pay such a dismally small rate of interest that it is hardly worth wasting money in savings accounts. One approach is to invest all of your capital in a diversified portfolio, knowing that you can sell anything and receive proceeds within one week.

Inflation Risk

A final form of risk important to mention is the risk of inflation. In the environment of the late 1990s, it was fashionable to believe that inflation was a thing of the past, but you may be assured that it will be back. Inflation, like all economic phenomena, is cyclical and tends to come and go on a predictable pattern. Only the timing and term of the pattern is uncertain. You need to select investments that exceed after-tax inflation, which is not always easy.

After-tax inflation is simple to compute. Your profits are reduced by your marginal tax rate, which should be calculated to include both federal and state income taxes. The remaining amount represents your after-tax net return. When this net return is compared to the current rate of inflation, it should be higher. If your after-tax return is exceeded by inflation, you are losing "real money" because of the double effect.

> **Example:** You invest $100 and earn $8 in one year. This is a gross return of 8 percent. Your combined federal and state tax rate is 40 percent, so that income tax takes $3.20 from your profit. The after-tax return is $4.80, or 4.8 percent. As long as inflation is lower than 4.8 percent, you have a true after-tax, after-inflation rate of return.

On the other side is inflation opportunity. Higher inflation normally translates to higher rates of return for investors. Thus, staying out of the market altogether erodes capital when inflation is high, effectively creating buying-power losses. So by being in the market and selecting investments that thrive during periods of inflation, you enjoy the inflation opportunity that is inherently found on the reverse side of inflation risk.

KEY POINT

Various forms of risk should be remembered when evaluating market risk, and all risk has a corresponding form of opportunity.

A Technician's View of the Market

How does the technician view risk? To many, the real game is all in forecasting. There is the risk of being wrong, meaning that investment decisions based on the forecast will result in losses. And there is the opportunity to be right as well, which leads to profits.

The technician is more concerned with price and with short-term and intermediate-term price movement than with long-term trends—not necessarily as a speculator, but with a particular point of view concerning price as the basis for investment decisions. Thus, the fundamentals are of little interest except to the degree that they confirm technical information. The technician believes that the study and analysis of market price is more interesting, valid, and revealing than the fundamentals, which are the financial statements and related profit and loss indicators that others follow.

Technicians believe in two principles as the basis for their point of view. The first belief is that the current price of a stock reflects all known information at the present time. This *efficient market theory* (see Chapter 2) is highly suspect in the chaotic world of overreaction and rumor that characterizes Wall Street, but this theory is at least a starting point. We can give some acceptability to it by assuming further that the overreactions of optimism and pessimism generally are offsetting to one another and that, therefore, the current price of a stock does reflect current knowledge plus perception of future value.

KEY POINT

The efficient market theory assumes that everything in the market works immediately and efficiently. It can be accepted only if we also assume that all inaccuracies are generally offsetting.

The second belief of the technician is that past information—fundamentals as well as price changes, volume, popularity of the stock, strength of the industry, and so forth—can be studied to predict future price patterns and movements. These two beliefs about market price serve as the basis for the technical point of view.

KEY POINT

The belief in predictability of the pattern of price movement in the future is a particular interpretation of trends and is unique to technical analysis.

Changing Your View with the Circumstances

There is no certain method to determine the accuracy of charting, price patterns, or future movement in prices by any interpretation. We can depend only on experience. The wise investor recognizes opportunity as one of the two risk-management techniques. Of equal importance is the second technique: recognizing errors and flaws in thinking, and then adjusting based on what has been learned.

In all forms of experience, it usually is not the initial error that causes problems (i.e., losses on investments) but the inability or unwillingness to change. For example, a technician might begin with a series of assumptions concerning price movement. Some of those assumptions are true and others are false. It is the ability to tell the difference and to act on that information that defines the successful investor.

Example: One investor tracks chart patterns in two different industries. He has observed a particular trading pattern that begins at the same time that interest rates begin to rise. This pattern anticipates by two or four weeks a drop in prices in utility stocks. The investor realizes that because utility stocks are interest-sensitive, the price pattern is valid as a technical indicator. He also understands that applying this conclusion to a different industry would not make sense.

KEY POINT

Indicators are not universal. A reliable stock price pattern that works in one set of circumstances has to be discounted in others until proven—or disproved.

On Being Right and Wrong

In the market, there is much emphasis on being right more often than the average investor. A measurement of success is the forecasting ability of a particular broker, analyst, or investor. But in reality, forecasting is only one skill (more accurately, a game) in the market. Is it really useful?

Forecasting—whether of stocks or of the weather—is of limited value. If you forecast rain for tomorrow but no one comes to the city with an umbrella, then your forecasting abilities are of no value. It would be better and more profitable to be right about the selection of a well-chosen stock than about tomorrow's movement in the DJIA.

KEY POINT

Forecasting is considered the "great game" of the market. Rather than being right about the future, however, you're better off being right about where to invest your money.

Most forecasting involves meaningless issues, at any rate—the favorite being the point level of the DJIA. But when you think about it, how does a future index level help you to decide which stocks to buy, hold, or sell today? The fact is, the DJIA is an interesting barometer of market interest and activity, but it tells you absolutely nothing about corporate profits, dividends, price changes on an individual basis, or the potential for future price changes. No, the real and valuable information about your investments, whether fundamental or technical, concerns specific stocks. The larger measurements of value are part of the forecasting game, and this is one reason that the Dow is so widely used. It is easily understood (although most people really do not know what it is, how it is computed, or what value, if any, it provides); it is easily reported in the financial press; and it makes for great speculation about the future because it is simple.

The Dow Jones Averages are explored in more detail in Chapter 5. While these averages serve as "the market" in many people's minds, they aren't really indicators at all. The index most popularly followed gives you nothing of any real value, either technical or fundamental, to help you with your investments.

The secret, of course, is to find those indicators that really do help. But first, as an investor, you need to understand how the averages were developed, and what they really mean.

CHAPTER 4

The Dow Jones Averages

To many investors, the market is the Dow Jones Industrial Average (DJIA). This average, consisting of 30 stocks out of thousands of publicly listed companies, represents only about one-fifth of the total market as measured by sales or profits; yet these companies do lead the market in many respects.

An appropriate measurement of some forms of market sentiment, the DJIA nonetheless represents only one version of what is going on. It does not tell us anything about new issues or their popularity, the way that our economy affects smaller companies, or the often subtle give and take of competition among industry leaders and runners-up. To really understand the market, we need to look closely at each individual company. The DJIA is *not* enough to tell you how to invest your money; to the contrary, the

KEY POINT

The DJIA reveals some forms of market sentiment, but it does not tell you how or when to buy, sell, or hold.

DJIA tells you nothing about the timing of your decisions. It only reflects an overall market sentiment.

What Is the Dow Jones Industrial Average?

The DJIA is not as comprehensive as the overall market. It measures one-fifth of the asset value of all publicly listed companies and, as a result, market sentiment about these leaders. Because the stocks in the DJIA are leading companies, they do lead the market.

The development of the DJIA was covered briefly in Chapter 3. In this chapter, more information is provided regarding the related transportation and utility averages as well as the composite of all three.

The DJIA is the primary technical indicator. It reflects the movement in prices of 30 of the largest listed companies, and because it reports only price movement, it is important to list the things that it reveals, as well as the things it does not reveal.

What the DJIA reveals:

- Collective price movement of 30 large companies
- A form of market sentiment reflected in prices
- Degrees of change in market sentiment measured by price

What the DJIA does not reveal:

- Price movement and other changes in the rest of the market
- Price movement for any particular stocks, even those in the DJIA
- Price movement in specific market sectors (e.g., finance)
- Market sentiment not measured by price alone
- Volume of the market
- Degrees of change in nonprice measurements of the market

As you can see, there is more to what the DJIA does not reveal than to what it does reveal. This is not a problem, however, if you view the DJIA for what it is: a general indicator that tells you a lot about price sentiments, current supply and demand, and mood. Remember, however, that short-term price change is not a valid or meaningful market indicator. This is one of the tenets of both the Dow Theory and the Random Walk Hypothesis. With both of the major philosophies about the market agreeing on the invalidity of current price movement, why is the DJIA so popular?

KEY POINT

Short-term price movement is unreliable as an indicator, and yet the DJIA is used as the major market indicator. This is ironic.

The DJIA is easy to understand, or so it is believed. In the financial press, it is easy to report that the market went up 30 points or fell 10 points. That is a simplified, easy to digest version of what is happening. And yet, it is not what is happening on the market at all. As an investor, you need to look beyond the reported market activity and concentrate on specific stocks and their technical and fundamental characteristics. Use the DJIA as an interesting mood indicator, but recognize that it is easy to allow yourself to be misled. Sentiment is not science. The DJIA not only ignores the fundamentals; it tells us absolutely nothing about future price changes, strength or weakness in the market, underlying moods, volume, or which stocks will rise and which ones will fall in value.

How the DJIA Works

The DJIA is used as a reporting mechanism in a world that requires simplistic answers. Unfortunately, it often is impossible to have both simplicity and accuracy. When such a conflict exists, the press—and the people—will choose simplicity almost every time.

KEY POINT

The DJIA reveals little, but it offers something that is easy to convey, which is a simplistic view of what is happening in the market.

The DJIA contains 30 stocks that, in the opinion of Dow Jones & Company, are representative of the overall market. Unfortunately for the investing public, the company does not publish its criteria for selecting stocks that are included on the average. They only state that companies are reviewed for their record of successful growth over time and popularity among investors. And the stocks on the DJIA are changed from time to time, so it should be troubling to anyone interested in accuracy that such changes occur at all. Why does one company cease to be more representative than another? Why is it removed? The latest change (as of 1999) occurred on March 17, 1997. Four companies were replaced at that time: Woolworth, Westinghouse-Electric, Texaco, and Bethlehem Steel were removed and replaced by Hewlett-Packard, Johnson & Johnson, Traveler's Group, and Wal-Mart. Why were these four companies considered better choices than the four they replaced? Perhaps more troubling to investors should be the question: What differences did these changes make in the DJIA itself? Did the change have a lot to do with the dramatic and sustained climb in the DJIA over a six-year period? And if so, then isn't the DJIA a form of manipulation of the market?

Such questions illustrate the point that depending too heavily on the DJIA as an indicator of the overall market can be misleading. It is not a forecasting tool, only an index of past direction for 30 stocks selected by one organization, and it is not a reflection of the market as a whole.

In an attempt to keep the DJIA as representative as possible—given the limitations imposed on the investing public by Dow Jones & Company—the averages are weighted. This means that

KEY POINT

In spite of what you hear in the financial press, the DJIA is not the market—it is only an index of 30 stocks.

some shares have more overall influence on the DJIA than others. Weighting occurs when stocks split, so that each company's typical "share of stock" has the same starting point or original weight.

This is necessary. For example, if three corporations are included on the DJIA from the same origin date, they start with a weighted average of 1.00 each. But if one of those companies has a stock split of 2 for 1, the investor ends up with twice as many shares, but each share has half of the original share value. This stock split also affects the stock's relative influence on an average. With twice the number of shares, but half the dollar value per share, it would no longer be accurate to compare one share of the split stock to one share of an unsplit stock.

Before weighting was used, the DJIA was computed very simply. Stock prices were added up and then divided by the number of stocks. In that regard, it truly was an "average," but as stocks split, that method became increasingly unreliable and inaccurate. The divisor has to be changed whenever stock splits occur.

Example: Three stocks are priced at $40, $50, and $60 per share. At first, the average is computed by adding these together and then dividing by 3:

$$\frac{40 + 50 + 60}{3} \ = \ 50$$

Then the $60 stock splits 2 for 1, creating twice as many shares, each at $30 per share. In order to maintain accuracy in this average, the divisor has to be changed to 2.4:

$$\frac{40 + 50 + 30}{2.4} = 50$$

The proper divisor was computed by adding together the post-split share values, and dividing that by the original average. In this case:

$$\frac{40 + 50 + 30}{50} = 2.4$$

This constant adjustment maintains accuracy in the average by ensuring that no stock split unfairly distorts the outcome. As a result of splits in many stocks, the weighting of each stock is different over time. Going back to our example, before the split the stocks in the simplified average were weighted as:

Price	Divisor	Weighting %
40	3	33.333
50	3	33.333
60	3	33.333

After the split, the weighting changed to:

Price	Divisor	Weighting %
40	2.4	33.333
50	2.4	41.670
30	2.4	25.000

Each time one stock splits, it affects the weighting of the companies in the average.[*] As of February, 1999, the 30 industrials in the DJIA had the following weightings:

Company	Weighting %
AlliedSignal Inc.	1.916
Aluminum Company of America	3.711

---

[*]The "weighting" of each stock in the DJIA refers to its relative influence on the whole, and should not be confused with "weighted average," as is used in some indexes. For example, some indexes multiply stock price by shares outstanding to arrive at a weighted average. The DJIA itself is not weighted.

American Express Co.	4.934
AT&T Corp.	3.833
Boeing Co.	1.638
Caterpillar Inc.	2.061
Chevron Corp.	3.532
Citigroup Inc.	2.646
Coca-Cola Co.	2.858
DuPont Co.	2.398
Eastman Kodak Co.	3.100
Exxon Corp.	3.039
General Electric Corp.	4.608
General Motors Corp.	3.808
Goodyear Tire & Rubber Co.	2.142
Hewlett-Packard Co.	3.245
International Business Machines Corp.	7.945
International Paper Co.	1.947
J.P. Morgan & Co.	5.120
Johnson & Johnson	3.861
McDonald's Corp.	3.828
Merck & Co.	3.627
Minnesota Mining & Manufacturing Co.	3.421
Philip Morris Cos.	1.838
Proctor & Gamble Co.	4.023
Sears, Roebuck & Co.	1.883
Union Carbide Corp.	1.905
United Technologies Corp.	5.510
Wal-Mart Stores, Inc.	3.984
Walt Disney Co.	1.596

The trouble with this weighting should be immediately apparent. IBM represents nearly 8 percent of the total DJIA, whereas Walt Disney Co. represents only about 1.5 percent. So if those two companies move in the same direction by the same amount, one—IBM—has about five times greater influence on the Dow than the other company. This is a problem.

Obviously, those stocks with the higher weighting—such as American Express, United Technologies, IBM, and J.P. Morgan (as of February, 1999)—have far greater influence on the average

KEY POINT

Because split stocks lose some degree of influence in the overall average, a stock that does not split but continues to grow in value over time, ends up with a distorted degree of influence on the averages, and thus, on the market.

than do the remaining 26 stocks, not to mention the thousands of stocks not included on the DJIA.*

For any four stocks to represent such a large portion of weighting on the DJIA begs the question. Even the most diligent attempt to make the DJIA as representative as possible still leaves us with an uncomfortable distortion of the "real" market represented by the more accurate, but much less interesting, composite of all listed stocks.

The Transportation Index

While the DJIA is the best known of the Dow Jones averages, it was preceded by that of transportation stocks. The Dow Jones Transportation Average (DJTA) was originated by Charles Dow in 1884, when it included nine railroad company stocks. When the DJIA was originated in 1896, Dow also expanded the "rail" list to 20 stocks, including two nonrail companies. As rail travel has diminished in influence, and airlines, trucking, and other forms of transportation have replaced it, the DJIA has expanded to include freight, trucking, airline, and shipping companies.

Today's list of 20 companies, complete with weighting,[†] is:

---

*At the end of February, 1999, these four companies represented 23.5 percent of the weighting on the DJIA. That is nearly one fourth of the entire influence of what most people consider the market.

†As of February, 1999.

Company	Weighting %
Airborne Freight	5.308
Alexander & Baldwin	2.509
AMR Corp.	7.244
Burlington Northern Santa Fe	4.218
CNF Transportation	5.261
CSX Corp.	5.010
Delta Air Lines	7.652
FDX Corp.	1.213
GATX Corp.	4.375
J.B. Hunt Transportation	3.042
Norfolk Southern	3.512
Northwest Airlines	3.277
Roadway Express	1.968
Ryder System	3.340
Southwest Airlines	3.943
UAL Corp.	7.934
Union Pacific	6.115
US Airways Group	6.178
USFreightways	4.265
Yellow Corp.	2.344

The Transportation Average has the same distortions as the DJIA. Three companies—AMR, Delta, and UAL—together represent 22.83 percent of the Transportation Average as of February, 1999. So 3 out of 20 stocks are said to represent more than one-fifth of the entire transportation market in terms of stock price movement. This is troubling in the same way that a few stocks dominating the DJIA is troubling. It shows the flaw in relying too heavily on averages and indexes.

The Utilities Index

The third of the three Dow Jones averages is the utilities average. This was added in January, 1929, and today consists of 15 stocks. An original purpose of the utilities average was to track changes in stock prices that reflected changes in interest rates, and utility companies are sensitive to interest rates.

The 15 stocks in the Dow Jones Utility Average (as of February, 1999) and their weighting are:

Company	Weighting %
American Electric Power	6.861
Columbia Energy Group	8.133
Consolidated Edison	7.652
Consolidated Natural Gas	8.974
Duke Energy	9.405
Edison International	4.146
Enron Corp.	10.730
Houston Industries	4.397
PECO Corp.	5.969
PG&E Corp.	5.108
Public Service Enterprise	6.220
Southern Co.	4.016
Texas Utilities	6.780
Unicom Corp.	5.789
Williams Cos.	5.749

As with the previous two averages, a few companies represent a significant portion of the utilities average. Duke and Enron together have weighting of 20.1 percent of the total, or one-fifth of the total average.

The Composite Average

The real problem of the averages comes when some stocks gain relatively more influence than the other stocks. For example, if a stock's price continues to rise over many years without stock splits, then its relative influence on the overall average becomes greater. This is demonstrated by the fact that among the three averages—industrial, transportation, and utility—only a few stocks exert about 20 percent overall, even when the combined averages are reviewed as a single entity.

This brings us to the Dow Jones Composite Average. This index is a combination of all the stocks on the New York Stock Exchange (NYSE). Movement in the Composite Averages represents change in the average share price during a trading day. Because this average includes all stocks, it might be viewed as more representative than any of the three smaller systems in use. However, the Composite Average does not make allowances for stock splits and similar influences. A more accurate measurement is the Wilshire 5000 Equity Index, which is reported in value-weighted dollars and shows value changes for 5,000 stocks.

Even with the alternatives, however, the most popular index to watch is the Dow, the industrial index of 30 stocks. Investors, it seems, are more interested in simplicity than accuracy, and this desire is aided directly by the financial press, whose desire for simplicity is greater still.

KEY POINT

Although more reliable and accurate measurements of the market are available, the Dow Jones Industrial Average has become the standard measure of the market. This in itself is revealing in terms of how the market actually works.

Other Ways to Measure the Market

Numerous methods have been developed for following all or part of the market. We discussed the major and best-known ones earlier in this chapter. One notable and popular index is the Standard & Poor's 500 (S&P 500), which reports on the 500 stocks that account for about nine-tenths of the total market value of stocks traded on the NYSE. Calculation of the S&P 500 is as follows: First, the price of each share is multiplied by the number of shares outstanding; next, the results are combined and reduced to an index value.

The Value of Averages

As Charles Dow realized 100 years ago, analyzing trends is an excellent way to measure the present and the past, and provides a tool for forecasting the future. Indexes and averages help us to reduce a high-volume, big-dollar market down to simple ratio form. The "number" value of the DJIA and other indexes represents a change over time from an arbitrary starting point of 100, zero, or some other number. Inflation is reported as a percentage, which is a calculation of the degree of change from one arbitrary level to another. The market index works in the same way.

The moving average is probably the most reliable form of average, because it can be manipulated to give greater weight to more recent information and less weight to older information. Even relatively complex averaging methods can be employed easily with automated calculation at your fingertips.

A simple average is computed easily: a) add up the values in the group being averaged, and b) divide the total by the number of values in the group. The result is a simple average.

Example: The following values are to be averaged: 336, 278, 256, and 442.

The formula for simple average is:

$$\frac{336 + 278 + 256 + 442}{4} = 328$$

A weighted moving average, as the name implies, gives greater value to more recent information. For example, let's use the same four values above but assume that 442 is the most recent. A weighted moving average might call for doubling the value of this latest information:

$$\frac{336 + 278 + 256 + 442 + 442}{5} = 350.8$$

Weighted moving averages can be calculated in other ways. For example, latest information can be given triple value.

Another method calls for weighting information in multiples. For example, the above field could be weighted four times for the most recent information; three times for the second most recent, twice for the third most recent, and only once for the oldest:

$$\frac{336 + 278 \ (2) + 256 \ (3) + 442 \ (4)}{10} = 342.8$$

The selection of the best weighting method depends on the volatility of the information being studied. If volatility is fairly low, then a simple moving average will suffice. In a *moving average*, the latest information is always incorporated into the average and the oldest information is dropped off. For example, if your moving average involves four values, it should always contain the most recent four values.

KEY POINT

Weighting a moving average gives greater value to more recent information, so that in addition to updating your analysis, the moving average also provides a valuable form of emphasis.

The longer the period studied, the more stable an average will appear. This is a valuable tool to be used in the study and forecasting of stocks. However, you also might decide that individually designed trend studies are of greater value to you than widely published averages, for reasons such as the following.

Everyone Else Has the Published Information, Too

What value is information that everyone else has, too? The real value of analysis and forecasting is the individual insight it provides you in the management of *your* portfolio, which is unrelated to the larger indexes and averages. You do not need the

> **KEY POINT**
>
> You should be skeptical about the value of any-
> thing that is shared universally, such as a published average.

DJIA to tell you how to manage your investments. This is fortu-
nate because the DJIA tells you absolutely nothing about your
individual stocks unless they are affected by the movement of the
30 industrials—and that is only a short-term issue.

Broad Indexes and Averages Are Too Nonspecific

The broader an average, the more reliable it is, that is if you are
interested in studying the entire market. But unless you teach a class
in investment theory, you need absolutely no interest in overall markets. What you need and want is information telling you whether to
buy, hold, or sell individual stocks, usually only a handful that interest you right now. So while the DJIA might be interesting and fun
to watch, and while it might provide you with a sense of the mood
in the market, it is not an analytical tool. It is an attractive icon on
the window of the market, but it is a shortcut to nowhere.

> **KEY POINT**
>
> Broad averages—involving the entire market or
> even 30 stocks—are of no real value to you in making
> investment decisions, unless you own shares of every stock
> in the average.

Reporting Price Movement Alone Is Unreliable

Averages generally are based on current prices of stocks,
which collectively are the equity dollar value of companies. But

this has nothing to do with future market price values. Averages reporting on current market value tell you nothing that is useful; as both the Dow Theory and the Random Walk Hypothesis conclude, short-term price movement is of no real value. In fact, emphasizing short-term price movement too much could be distracting as well as unproductive.

> ## KEY POINT
>
> Price movement is only one of many indicators, and not always the most important. Other factors, such as volume, interest rates, strength of the industry, and competitive position of the company, to name a few, might be far more important.

No Trend Analysis Is Feasible Using Short-Term Reporting

There exists no trend analysis that you can apply using day-to-day price movements. What value can you take from seeing that the Dow rose 80 points yesterday? Or fell 50 points today? It is true that individual stocks, including yours, might react to these movements by following suit for the moment, but these fluctuations tend to even out over time (as moving averages will show). And when you consider movements in averages, what do they tell you? How do they help you to decide what to do in your portfolio? Averages deal in short-term reporting and provide no analytical

> ## KEY POINT
>
> Any indicator on which you rely for making investment decisions should provide you with information that actually is related to your portfolio—without exception.

information whatsoever. You can learn much more by concentrating on the particular trends—both fundamental and technical—shown in the stocks you own or are thinking of owning.

Problems with Averages and Indexes

Even if you develop your own tracking devices and you are comfortable with them, you still need to manage the problems associated with the use of trend analysis. Your own averages or indexes might provide you with very nice reporting, but you still need to develop a level of skill in interpretation.

> ## KEY POINT
>
> Even the most skilled analyst has to answer one salient question when all is said and done: What conclusion should I draw and what actions are mandated by my conclusions?

Every analyst, whether working for a big Wall Street firm or working in a den at home, has to face this reality at some point. The task of managing investments is not simply the tracking of stocks and the timing of buying and selling, but involves a much broader point of view. Analysis provides us with information, but of what quality and dependability? What good is a moving average if you do not also know what signals it should fire?

The essence of managing your investments is not just developing a tracking system, but tying that system to a predetermined series of decisions. Investors need to set goals. These goals are guideposts for investment decisions. For example, a goal strictly related to the decision to buy, hold, or sell might be expressed in the following manner:

I will continue to hold this stock unless my upside goal is met, or unless my downside bail-out position is met. I will sell if and when the stock rises by 25 percent or more above its purchase price (net of commissions) and continues to rise. When it has stopped rising for three consecutive trading sessions, I will sell. If the stock's value falls to 20 percent below the purchase price, I will consider that a bail-out position and will sell immediately.

The determination and definition of buy, sell, and hold ranges—and of the price-related changes that also influence the decision—can be determined by any number of fundamental or technical considerations, including price movement as well as other matters. Price movement can be tracked strictly on a percentage basis with percentage ranges picked as a matter of individual comfort zone; or they may be predetermined based on chart analysis and the careful study of resistance and support levels (see Chapter 5).

KEY POINT

The purpose of trend analysis is to provide you with an intelligent method for making important decisions about your investments.

The investor who manages a portfolio through trend analysis has one-half of the task under control. More is needed, though: the means for making a decision based on predefined goals that are followed faithfully and self-imposed rules for buying, holding, and selling that are adhered to regularly. This is how successful investors operate, by avoiding the temptation to act out of greed or other emotions rather than pursuing a smart course that has been mapped out well in advance.

It might be an ultimate irony about investing that the DJIA is the universally acknowledged bellwether of market sentiment, mood, security, perception, and opinion—when, in fact, it provides no meaningful information on which to base such matters. What, then, should be used to develop our own personal sentiments?

On an individual basis, of course, it is the outcome of recent investment decisions that determines our attitude. If you profit from your timing and selections, you will tend to be happy about the market, feeling upbeat and optimistic; if you lose money, you might be bitter, anxious, fearful, and pessimistic. In fact, your individual mood might be at variance with the majority—more often than not.

The value of having averages and indexes also might explain their long-standing popularity. They provide investors with a sense of community, a sense of the mood in the market as reflected by current price trends in the 30 industrials. We always should remember that this is a perception only and might have little to do with the future. It has been demonstrated many times that the current mood of the market—good or bad—might be completely unjustified by events that are about to occur, most notably performance of the stocks in your own portfolio.

Because we cannot know with certainty what price movements will occur in the future, perhaps the real value of the DJIA is found in the connection it gives us with the rest of the market. As an astute investor, you can learn a lot by observing this as the primary value, and then acting and reacting to changes based on analysis you do of your own portfolio.

Averages and Indexes as Tools— And Nothing More

Every investor needs to recognize analytical tools, like averages and indexes, for what they are: limited indicators only. Ultimately, your decisions cannot be made on the basis of a pat formula, or strictly in response to recent change. There is a tendency in the market to want to find easy answers and to develop systems that are flawless. But in practice, no such systems exist.

All of the study you perform about averages, including the most sophisticated application involving weighting, moving averages, and on-going analysis, really does not tell you what actions to take, or when to take them. You really need to establish goals for yourself and then act according to those goals. Every goal should be based upon a few fundamental attributes, which are: risk tolerance, personal economics, well-understood perceptions about your own future, and—most of all—change.

Risk Tolerance

All investors struggle with the definition of their own ideas about how much risk is appropriate. No one else can answer this question for you because no two people's circumstances are identical. In addition, someone else with similar circumstances might be willing to take greater risks, or willing to accept lower rewards. Risk tolerance is one side of the coin. The other side is earnings potential. Remember that the two sides are unavoidably related. The greater the potential for big profits, the greater the risk. And the lower the risk, the less potential is associated with that strategy for earnings.

In setting your goals, you begin by defining your own risk tolerance. If you believe you want to take great risks in search of high profits, then you need to also understand that you stand to lose greater amounts of capital as well. There is no such thing as a risk-free, high-potential investment (in spite of what some promoters will tell you). While every reader of this book knows this, it bears stating the fact specifically, because it is

KEY POINT

Everyone needs to think about the risks in the market. Thinking only of the rewards is too easy—and too dangerous.

easy to act contrary to what we actually know. The market, in many respects, is like a Hall of Amnesia, which we walk through making mistakes when we should have known better, and where such mistakes are only seen when we turn and look backward.

Personal Economics

The second factor in setting personal investment goals is your current economic situation. Every investor has to be realistic about today's economics. When families start out, earnings are generally low, perhaps too low to begin an earnest diversified program of the scope you would like. The temptation in this case is to betray your risk tolerance level in an attempt to get something going, even when it is not appropriate.

It is important to set investment goals that are not so ideal that they cannot be put into practice right away. The goal has to conform to the circumstances. For example, you might need to establish a diversified portfolio that will create steady long-term growth to save for a child's college education. If you don't have enough capital to diversify today, you need to find an acceptable alternative that meets your risk tolerance standards, meets the financial requirements stated in your personal goal, and does not risk capital that you cannot afford to lose.

KEY POINT

Goal setting is not merely a way to "make money" in the market. The goal has to conform to the realities of your situation; otherwise, your goal won't work for you.

Perceptions of the Future

It is particularly interesting that so many investors don't really think in terms of the future. They are preoccupied with today's stock prices and predictions. This may occur even among people who see themselves as forward looking, as people who work from goals. In reality, the kinds of actions you take in the market are determined by how you view the future, whether you are aware of it or not. Your perceptions affect your level of optimism and your ability and willingness to tolerate risk.

In setting goals, remember to look beyond the analytical tools available to you today. It is easy to become caught up in the mathematical study of trends, and to forget to overlay those tools with a sense of self. Every investor has her own ideas about where the economy is heading, what future earnings will be, and how future investing will add to retirement and lifestyle security.

KEY POINT

Your perceptions about the future may influence how you invest than does any other factor—even a confirmed trend.

Change

The one certainty about the future is that your perception of it is going to change. We tend to think in terms of goals, and, as healthy and well-advised as that is, we cannot really know what the future holds. So too much emphasis on trend analysis is flawed if only because it is impossible to know what will happen tomorrow or next year.

Influences outside of the market have as much to do with change as do influences within the market. So the study of current trends based on market data is flawed from its very beginning. Considerations like marriage, divorce, death, purchase or sale of a home, birth of a child, change in career—to name a few of the big ones—will not only change what you are going to be able to do in the future, but will also change your priorities.

KEY POINT

Change is the only sure thing. So any goals established today will not only be inaccurate, they will also be unimportant as priorities change.

CHAPTER 5

Charting Basics

A look backward is always revealing. History is crystal clear, but looking forward is not quite as easy. Putting it another way, forecasting is always easier when we forecast the past than when we try to forecast the future.

A chartist is a person who believes that market price ranges can be predicted by studying recent stock trading patterns, and that stocks trade in predictable ranges and patterns. It would be a simple matter if we could combine predictable patterns with timing of those patterns, but false stops and starts characterize the patterns of trading. Some fundamentalists, dedicated to the long term, completely discount the value of charting—the tracking of stock prices—in favor of more solid financial indicators. We come back to the old question of the reliability of short-term trading as a prediction tool. Remember, Charles Dow's observations

KEY POINT

Chartists believe that recent trading patterns can be used to anticipate future price movement. This belief has to be qualified.

as incorporated into the Dow Theory and the basics of the Random Walk Hypothesis both point to short-term trading patterns as unreliable and meaningless.

The problem encountered by many chartists is that their hindsight is always perfect; thus, they try to apply the logic of past observation to future price change as well. This is more easily said than done. We discover upon analysis that patterns do not always repeat themselves and that there might just be a certain randomness to the way that prices change from moment to moment. Using a more reliable and longer-term moving average, we begin to see a long-term pattern emerging in a stock's price tendencies, or a real trend. The trend shows that, indeed, longer-term price movement is predictable based on fundamental analysis, that predictions about financial strength do translate to a predictable growth in market value, and that short-term fluctuation does not matter if you are holding a stock for the long term.

Even so, chartists have a point. Some of the observations concerning patterns and price ranges do translate into reliable *intermediate* indicators that can be helpful in identifying likely future change in a stock's price. Everyone is familiar with the simple adage "Buy low and sell high," but in fact, there should be a second part to the saying: "instead of the other way around." As any chartist will tell you, if you look backward at the trading patterns of a stock, the best points to buy and to sell are identified easily. However, there is a tendency for people to sell when a stock is low, and to buy when it is high. The chartist is able to observe the irony of this tendency and to avoid it, if the same chartist learns from the patterns.

KEY POINT

The idea to "buy low and sell high" is all well and good—but investors tend to do just the opposite.

Why is it that investors do the opposite of what they should? In two words: panic and greed. When an investor owns a stock and its value begins to fall, there is a tendency to panic and to dump the stock before more money is lost. Thus, panic causes people to sell low. At such times, the idea of buying more stock is unthinkable. The investor is acting out of panic, not out of calculated or strategic thinking.

On the opposite side, investors buy when a stock is high, and the closer to the peak, the greater the buying activity tends to be. Investors see a stock rising and sense that they are losing out on the feast, so they buy the stock even though it may be at an all-time high. We see this trend over and over. In fact, this is why charting makes some sense. It enables you to recognize the trading patterns and to ignore the tendency toward panic and greed.

There is another old saying about the market that is worth remembering in relation to greed: "There is room in the market for bulls and there is room for bears. But there is no room for pigs." In other words, greed—like panic—is not a wise part of your strategy. It ensures that money will be lost. Successful investors are able to step back and analyze a situation and do not tend to go along with the current popular thinking, which invariably is wrong.

KEY POINT

Going along with the majority is an easy and comfortable position. But remember, the majority is usually wrong. In the market, the herd mentality is a losing mentality.

If you want to use charting wisely, then let go of the idea that it can be used as a tool to actually predict price movement. That is impossible no matter what forms of analysis you use. The real value in charting is to help you to gain and keep perspective on what is going on in the market, and especially in individual stocks, at any particular moment. A trading pattern does not necessarily indicate where a stock's price is going, but it does show you where it is in relationship to its past trading pattern. And that is where some charting concepts become valuable analytical tools.

What Charting Reveals

Charting is directly opposed to the Random Walk Hypothesis, at least in some respects. Remember, proponents of the Random Walk Hypothesis contend that all stock price movement is entirely random and arbitrary, that market prices overreact, and that there are so many influences at work that it is impossible to know in advance what is going to occur. The pure chartist argues that studying past price movement reveals and predicts everything quite precisely. While neither belief can be proved scientifically (or otherwise), each side has its faithful followers and each side is attacked by skeptics. In truth, though, the market is quite random at times, while at other times it seems orderly and predictable. If you use a specific time frame to try to prove a point in support of one belief or the other, then you do not really have a scientific sample.

The chartist has advantages over the less visual skeptic of charting. The chart shows recent historical trading patterns that can reveal at a glance how volatile a stock has been, which is a potentially valuable piece of information. The historical analysis of long-term trading tendencies also might reveal that some long-term cycles have been in play for a stock over many years. Stocks tend to experience periods of popularity or unpopularity with investors, and patterns might emerge from these tendencies or cycles.

KEY POINT

Charts show changes not only in price and price range, but also in volatility.

For most uses, however, short-term and intermediate-term analysis of charts is more likely to show the trading ranges between the wave crests and bottoms. Some stocks trade in very narrow ranges, while other, more volatile stocks have more broadly ranging patterns over time. These are the more interesting stocks for chartists because of the constant price movement.

KEY POINT

Volatile stocks, those with broader than average trading ranges, are far more interesting to watch than narrower-band stocks. The more volatile issues also offer the greater market risks.

What Charting Does Not Reveal

In summarized form, charting does *not* reveal one very important piece of information: the future price of the stock. It reveals neither the price nor anything about the timing of an investment decision. The trading pattern has two elements, both of which are of critical importance. First is the price level itself. Second, but often discounted or overlooked, is the timing. You might be correct in guessing that a stock's market price will go from $35 to $40 per share, but so what? This information is of little value unless you also predict *when* that change will occur. Should I put my money into the stock now? Or should I wait for ten years? And one more question: Will it go to $40 per share directly, or will it first dip down to $25 per share?

When you begin asking such questions, you realize that simple prediction is a troubling art. You might predict that the temperature outside will go to 90 in the shade, but when will that occur? The chartist is going to be right some of the time in forecasting a particular range of prices for stocks under study. Why? Because

KEY POINT

Prediction is of no value unless the timing of the outcome also can be identified.

some trading patterns can be predicted. But charts do not tell you a number of things, such as

- whether the stock you are interested in will trade in the same pattern as another stock;
- whether the changes will occur quickly or take many years;
- whether the *degree* of change will be consistent with past patterns; and
- whether intermediate and opposing change will occur before the predicted change.

In other words, there are many unknown variables even when the forecaster is correct. Even in the more certain environment of business forecasting, the budget might follow the general tendency correctly, but everyone knows that the precise timing of income, costs, and expenses cannot be controlled completely. Unforeseen outside influences might change the entire set of assumptions—and in fact, they can be relied on to do so.

Tracking Device or Forecasting Tool?

Should the chart be used as a method for forecasting future price ranges or as a device for tracking alone? If used for forecasting, the chart is presumed to be recording changes that somehow predict the future with enough precision to be taken seriously. If used for tracking alone, it serves no analytical value other than for historical interest.

We propose, instead, that the combination of tracking and forecasting can help to make charting a valuable tool for the management of your portfolio. It is a flawed concept that trading patterns alone have some predictive value, because there is a well-under-stood random element to short-term price change. Proponents of both the Dow Theory and the Random Walk Hypothesis agree that short-term trends have no value in analysis. This is true of any form of analysis. A momentary change in value from a prior value tells you nothing. However, when trading ranges are studied in light of repetitive patterning and used in combination with other analytical systems, charting cannot be ignored.

KEY POINT

Tracking price movement for change in price alone is mundane. What is truly interesting is what the patterns reveal about what will happen next.

Remember, the entire purpose of analysis is to develop and recognize trends. If you are able to recognize patterns in trading—especially repetitive patterns—then you also might be able to anticipate future price movements in the short term to a fairly accurate degree. You attempt to forecast not the exact price, but a reasonable and likely range of prices. The idea of price ranging is essential to understanding the real purpose of charting. The chartist follows a stock's price in terms of its *trading range*, looking for patterns of *support* (meaning the minimum approximate price a stock is likely to fall to) and *resistance* (meaning the maximum approximate price a stock is likely to rise to), and for *breakout* events (when a stock's price falls below support level or rises above resistance level) to identify critical changes in trading range. The breakout, by itself, might merely redefine the trading range or, if it persists, repeats, and magnifies, it could signal a major change in perception of the company.

In order to track a stock's price, you need to know its daily trading range as well as closing price. Knowing the trading range might help you anticipate breakouts. For example, if a stock generally trades in a narrow range, say, a half point or less, and suddenly begins wider swings of four to five points daily, that signifies a lot of interest and activity in the stock. This is highly visible on a chart if you are tracking all three important forms of information: closing price, high for the day, and low for the day. Of course, you want all of this information in a presentation format that makes it easy to absorb.

Chart Types

The type of chart you select should clearly display the kind of information you need in order to achieve a quick, visual summary of the stock's movement. While a single day's movements might not be important in isolation, the movements of a series of days, weeks, and months can be revealing. As such a tool, what should your chart reveal?

Several methods are available; however, the bar chart provides you with the most useful format for tracking everything you need. Remember, though, if the chart's graphics are overly complex, then their real value and purpose is lost.

Bar Charts

A simple bar chart summarizes a stock's price range each day. Figure 5.1 shows how a simple bar chart is constructed. The range from high price to low price is reflected in the vertical line for each day.

A problem with the simple bar chart is that it shows the range but not the closing price of the stock. An alternative type of chart is the closing-price bar chart. By adding a small horizontal line, you can view not only the daily high and low, but also the closing price. Figure 5.2 shows how the closing-price bar chart looks.

To view your charts with a long-term perspective, consider adding a moving average line for closing prices. Construct your moving average using weighting if you wish, and be sure that

FIGURE 5.1 Simple Bar Chart

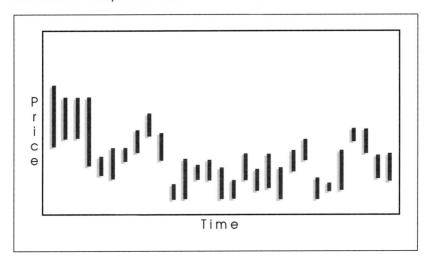

FIGURE 5.2 Closing-Price Bar Chart

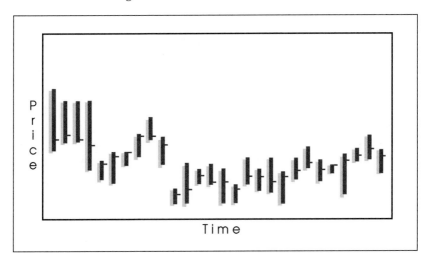

the average provides some meaningful data; otherwise, drop it from your charting analysis. Figure 5.3 shows how a moving average might look when added to the bar chart. For purpose of this illustration, assume a three-day moving average without any weighting.

FIGURE 5.3   Closing-Price Bar Chart with Moving Average

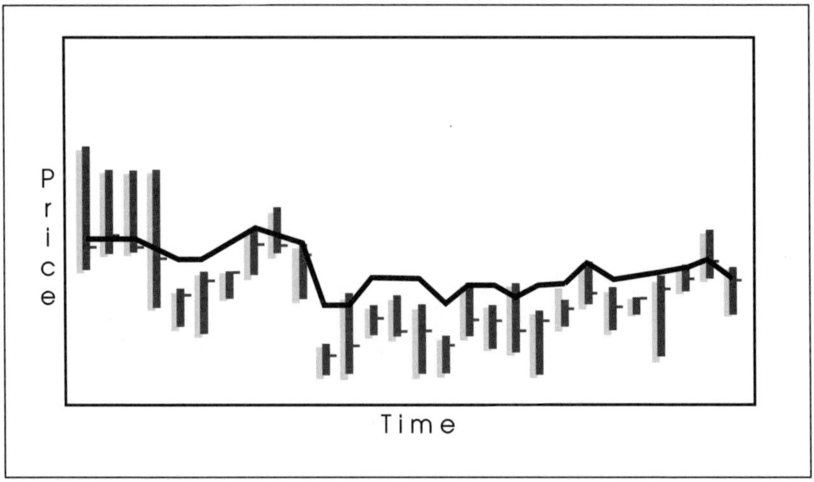

Patterns and Their Value

In any cycle, certain patterns of change repeat themselves; thought not always in the same manner or degree and, more to the point, rarely with the same timing. The chartist might be very accurate in anticipating future price change patterns, but specifying when and how those patterns will occur is a more difficult task.

In the market, stocks experience overall and generalized tendencies that can be observed in simplified patterns. Figure 5.4 shows these tendencies. The illustration on the left shows a classic tendency beginning with a bull movement (1) and ending with a bear movement (3). The middle, horizontal, section (2) shows the separating phase. The illustration on the right shows the same pattern, but with a bear trend leading the way, followed by a reversing bull trend.

Often people think of stocks as rising sharply and then falling; or falling sharply and then bouncing back. While this might appear to be the case—and often is in short-term movements—it rarely happens in primary trend movements. The classic pattern includes a separation between two opposing movements.

FIGURE 5.4 Primary Cycle Movements

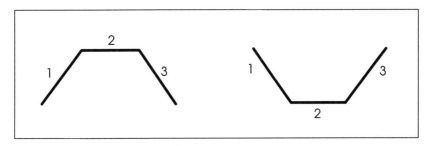

![KEY POINT]

KEY POINT

Stock price patterns do not always conform to our preconceived notions. A common tendency shows periods of change interspersed with periods of relative inactivity.

Head and Shoulders

While the overall tendencies of the market provide us with a "big picture" view of how prices change, they do not anticipate future directions of change. The only certainty is that some patterns are likely to be repeated over the long term. One reliable shorter-term pattern is called *head and shoulders* because of its shape. Figure 5.5 shows a typical head and shoulders pattern in price change.

The three emphasis lines show why this pattern is called head and shoulders. The first and third lines represent the shoulders, and the middle line represents the head. The head and shoulders pattern occurs frequently, notably as market movements top out or bottom out for a stock. The head is a final rally for a stock, with a pre- and post-rally tendency (shoulders). If the pattern occurs at the end of a bull trend, it is said to be a strong predictive indicator that a bear pattern is about to begin. Head and shoulders is the detailed version of a market top.

FIGURE 5.5   Head and Shoulders

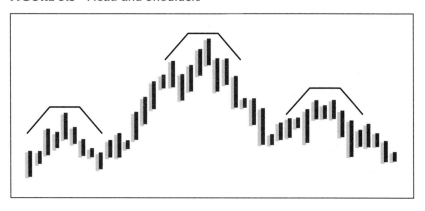

FIGURE 5.6   Inverse Head and Shoulders

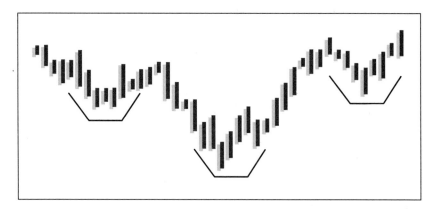

The same thing happens in reverse at the bottom of a stock's bear trend, and anticipates a bull tendency. This is called the inverse head and shoulders, which is illustrated in Figure 5.6. Note that the same emphasis lines identify the shoulders and the head, with the second and final shoulder depicting the last decline at the beginning of a bull tendency.

These patterns—in fact, all patterns worthy of study—should be analyzed in combination with a careful analysis of trading volume. Remember that stock price by itself does not always tell the whole story. If volume changes dramatically during pattern development, it could work as a confirming factor; if volume does not increase all that much, it could be a sign that the apparent pattern is false and should not be used as a signal to change investment strategy.

KEY POINT

Besides changes in price and pattern, you will do well to track volume and other helpful trends. The more information available, the better.

The typical trading pattern represented by the head and shoulders should be confirmed in some way. At times, the head and shoulders pattern seems to point to a change in direction, but the price is unable to break through its previously established range—support on the downside or resistance on the upside. All important changes in a stock's price involve a breakout from previously established trading ranges. The support and resistance levels of a stock, and corresponding breakout patterns, are illustrated in Figure 5.7.

Note the numerous minor head and shoulders patterns that occur immediately before each breakout. While this is not a dependable or consistent pattern, it is typical. The tendency within the pattern is to test the resistance or support levels before going through them. This does not mean to imply a sentient nature to stock prices; the movement of a stock does not itself have a consciousness to it (although it is easy to fall into the trap of believing that it does). But the testing of resistance and support levels does occur on a conscious level on the part of institutional managers and individuals who buy and sell shares in the subject company; on the part of the company's management, which takes actions that affect the stock; and among analysts, whose predictions future price levels are based not only on fundamentals, but also on trading patterns.

FIGURE 5.7 Support and Resistance

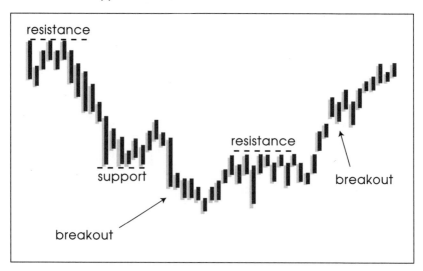

KEY POINT

Stock prices do not have conscious knowledge of their own movement, but when you follow the market, it is easy to come to believe that they do.

Double Top and Double Bottom

Support and resistance can be characterized by a pattern similar to head and shoulders called the *double top* and *double bottom*. This is two peaks (on the top) with a valley in between, as illustrated in Figure 5.8. The double top—especially if accompanied by heavy volume—is said to indicate an imminent strong reversal. Thus, as Figure 5.8 shows, a two-part test of resistance level that fails to break through could anticipate a bear trend.

The reverse is true of the double bottom, as shown in Figure 5.9. If support level is tested twice—again, with heavy volume—

FIGURE 5.8 Double Top

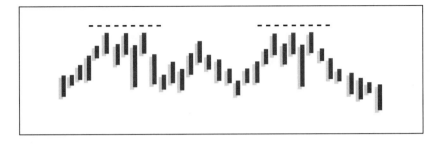

FIGURE 5.9 Double Bottom

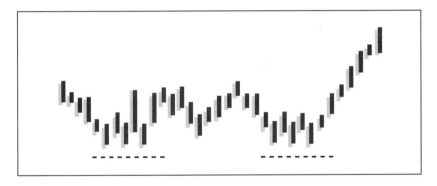

without breaking through, the pattern is believed to forecast a reversing bull trend.

The actual degree of resistance to the price level identified by the term *resistance* is a matter of opinion. The term is used to delimit the typical trading range as established by the current and prior patterns. A breakout is the significant event that, if confirmed and sustained, signals a change in direction. Stock prices tend to operate within a defined range (which is different for each stock), but it is rare to see widely divergent trading ranges of 20, 30, or 40 points. An intermediate-term trading range of 10 points or less is more typical than one with a lot of change between high and low prices.

The same argument is true of support levels. Stocks do not tend to dip deeply into low territory and then go to vastly higher highs on a consistent basis. The interaction of supply and demand tends to stabilize resistance and support into a fairly narrow range. It cannot be specifically stated that 10 points is a normal or typical range, but such a range is not unusual over a period of several weeks to several months.

KEY POINT

The head and shoulders pattern is a classic demonstration of support and resistance.

Many patterns, such as head and shoulders or double top or bottom, confirm breakouts when they do occur and, of greater interest, might actually predict a breakout before it occurs. Again, the problem for the chartist is not the pattern identification but the timing. This is why you need to track not only the pattern, but the length of time involved in past patterns *and* any changes in corresponding trading volume. These three elements—trading price range, volume, and time—are the tools you must study together to make your charts valuable.

KEY POINT

It is a mistake to limit your analysis to any one element, such as price. You must study volume and time as well as price to really recognize a price pattern.

The Broadening Formation

The broadening formation illustrates a tendency for prices to change over time so that the trading range grows vertically. The

FIGURE 5.10 The Broadening Formation

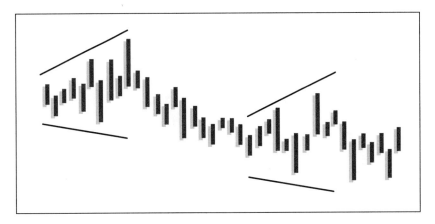

increased volatility associated with a broadening of the trading range is often accompanied by changes in volume, as you might expect. If the price is trending downward, meaning the broadening effect is lowering the support level, it could indicate the emergence of a bear trend. And if the broadening is raising the resistance level, then it could be interpreted as a sign of an imminent rally for that stock. The broadening formation is illustrated in Figure 5.10.

The Triangle and Its Variations

A related pattern is called the *triangle*. This pattern, illustrated in Figure 5.11, is the inverse of a broadening formation. It is less reliable as an indicator of future price breakout because with an ever-diminishing trading range, it cannot be known which way price will move—it is only certain that a breakout will occur, because the range cannot diminish forever.

A variation of the triangle formation is called *flags and pennants*. This pattern represents a pause in a trend, witnessed by the price changes following periods when the flags and pennants are observed. Figure 5.12 shows the typical flags and pennants formation. When this period concludes, most chartists believe that it serves as a confirmation of the direction of

FIGURE 5.11   The Triangle

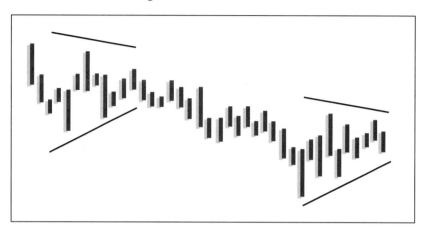

FIGURE 5.12   Flags and Pennants

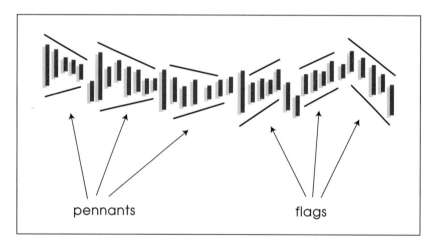

pennants   flags

KEY POINT

Flags and pennants—like so many patterns in charts—are open to interpretation. And hindsight is always more accurate than foresight.

longer-term movement. (Of course, if the stock finishes the flags and pennants period and then continues its previous direction, then this belief is validated.) However, prices also might take a reverse direction following a flags and pennants series, so, as with all charting analysis, nothing is certain. But the flags and pennants patterns for particular stocks with repetitive charting patterns can be revealing about the phases and direction of price movement.

Still another variation of the triangle is the *wedge*. Like the triangle, the wedge is characterized by a narrowing price range. Prices might be rising within the wedge pattern or falling. When the price range is on the rise, the pattern shows an inability of the stock to break through the resistance level created by the modified shape, which often is taken as a sign that future price patterns will be bearish. When prices finally fall below the established wedge support level, it is taken as a sell signal. When the wedge declines in its trend, the opposite arguments are true. The price does not break through the support level created by the falling wedge, and, when prices rise above the created pattern, this acts as a buy signal. These patterns are summarized in Figure 5.13.

FIGURE 5.13   The Wedge

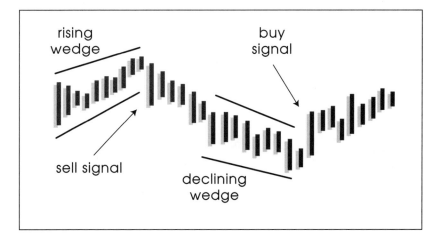

Gaps

The *gap* is a frequently seen pattern in charts of a stock. It is a condition in which the trading range from one day to the next contains a gap in the prices. The *common gap* is illustrated in Figure 5.14.

The study of the gap can be revealing. A common gap is minor and has no importance or significance. It involves relatively minor price differences between trading ranges and occurs within an existing trading range. No change in the direction of price movement should be expected. However, a *breakaway gap* has more importance to the chartist. Not only is it a separation, but it also moves the stock price into territory with no near-term price activity. If the gap is not "filled" with price activity consolidating new and prior ranges within a short time—a few days—it is a very strong signal that a bull trend is

FIGURE 5.14   The Common Gap

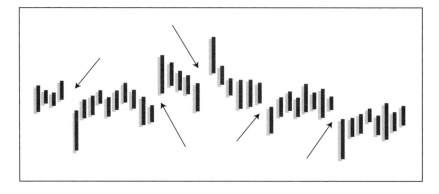

KEY POINT

A gap is particularly interesting because it is a break in what was previously an orderly trend. A gap might anticipate a significant and sudden change.

FIGURE 5.15   Gap Formation

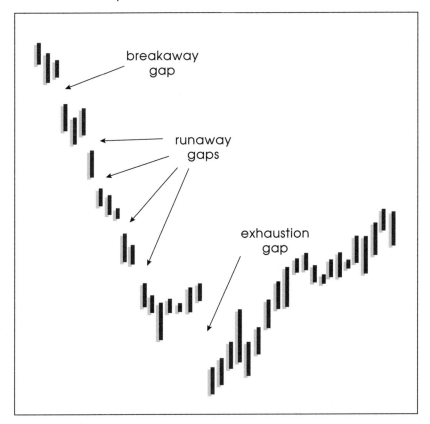

underway (for rising gaps) or that a bear trend is underway (for falling gaps).

A *runaway gap* is an acceleration in the breakaway pattern. Typically, runaway patterns occur one after another in strong movement periods. The established pattern signals its end with an *exhaustion gap*, a relatively large gap in the established direction, to be followed shortly by a reversal in the direction of change. These types of gaps are illustrated in Figure 5.15.

Spiking

A spike occurs when the top of a trading range is considerably higher than on the day before or after (*spike high*), or when a range's

FIGURE 5.16   Spiking

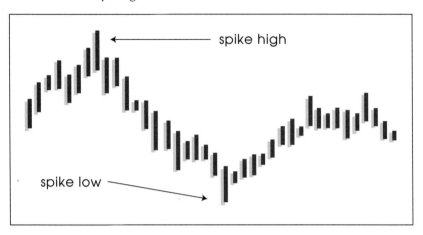

low point is considerably lower than on the surrounding days (*spike low*). Both of these patterns are illustrated in Figure 5.16.

These spikes might act as signals in certain circumstances, notably if a spike high follows a series of rises or a spike low follows a series of falls in the price pattern, in which case the spike might indicate the limit of buying or selling pressure. To evaluate spikes, you need to consider the distance between the prior day's high and the spike, the degree of price increase in the stock preceding the spike day, and where the stock closes on the spike day. For spike highs, if the stock closes near the low of the trading range, it is a strong signal that the stock will then begin a period of decline. Conversely, for spike lows, if the stock closes near the high range of the spike day, it signifies a likely bull trend in following days.

Reversal Days

The *reversal day* pattern is a standard formation in which a day's trend opposes the previously established trend. This is a common pattern due to the workings of supply and demand. As prices rise, more holders want to take their profits, translating to selling pressure; as prices fall, stocks become attractive to more would-be investors, translating to buying pressure. Because

KEY POINT

Interpretation of patterns in isolation is a futile exercise. Virtually all indicators have to be confirmed or act as confirmation points for independent, separate indicators to have validity.

reversals are common and characteristic of most trading patterns and vary only by degree, how can they help us to interpret a chart? Generally speaking, to signify a true reversal, a new high (or new low) must be established. In a reversal high day pattern, a new high in the trading of the stock occurs, and the stock then closes below the prior day's closing price. For a reversal low day, the stock first experiences a new low, followed by a close above the previous day's closing price. Reversal within a trading range, by itself, is not significant. But when coupled with the connection to a new high (or a new low), it is very significant. The high in such cases is thought to represent the high point in a rising price trend (reversal high), and the low is thought to represent the low point in a declining trend (reversal low). These points are illustrated in Figure 5.17.

FIGURE 5.17   Reversal Days

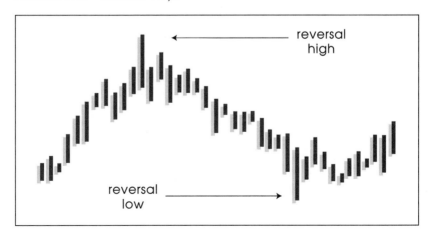

KEY POINT

Even a clearly identified and predictable trading pattern—if there is such a thing—cannot be applied among different stocks. Every stock will follow its own trend, without relationship to other stocks' patterns.

An awareness of the various trading patterns and the common beliefs about what they reveal can be instructive. This must be accompanied by the observation that not every stock demonstrates a similar cycle; thus, the trading patterns might be completely different. Even if you accept the premise that a "normal" trading reaction to a charting signal should be expected, there are no guarantees. The price movement of each company is unique, and price movement in short-term patterns is more random than we would like. Still, patterns provide some means for analysis and comparison and should not be ignored. To the contrary, the chart is, at the very least, an excellent form of confirmation for other signals.

Automated Charting Resources

Developing your own charts requires several steps: finding daily information about the trading high and low and the close for each and every day; placing this information on a chart to scale; and then studying the results, including development of your own moving average. But all of this is not necessary.

You can find ample resources on the Internet to help with your charting needs. Some are available by subscription only, whereas others will allow you free access to updated charting information. If you happen to invest in a stock tracked by one or more of these services, then you have available a *Favorite* of considerable value. A favorite is a saved Web page that can be retrieved easily with a click of your mouse. Favorites are organized into categories for ease of access. For example, you might create an investing folder and store all of your favorite research and information sites under that folder. Check out the following:

Barchart.com	www.stocks.barchart.com
By the Horns	avidinfo.com/bear
Decision Point	www.decisionpoint.com
Equis	www.equis.com
Liberty Research	www.libertyresearch.com
Charting Software	www.chartingsoftware.com/education.htm

Charting Price and Volume Together

Discussion about the market price of a stock, which occupies a good deal of time among analysts and investors, is only part of the whole story. A lot can be learned by also tracking volume.

The daily volume can be revealing, especially as a signal of impending change. As a general rule—and remember, this is only a general rule—both price and volume patterns tend to be consistent until changes are imminent. So it is often true that a change in price is anticipated by sudden growth in volume. Such growth can characterize buying or selling pressure, so the number of shares traded is only part of the total picture. You also need to determine whether volume represents upside volume—activity created by an influx of buyers, or downside volume—activity created by an influx of sellers. Careful analysis of early signs is important because these changes can and do occur quickly.

KEY POINT

Careful study of volume is essential to anticipate price movement; reaction to volume changes often is rapid and immediate.

The kinds of changes you can see in hindsight generally involve sudden and large changes in volume, far above typical daily levels, immediately followed by sudden changes in price levels, up or down. Of course, price changes might occur concurrently with changes in volume or immediately afterward. In other words, once you see the obvious change in volume, it probably is too late to act before everyone else.

Some advance signs might be available if you look for them carefully in your study of volume and price trends. Combinations of some trading patterns, as discussed earlier in this chapter, with subtle changes in corresponding volume, could foretell big price changes far in advance of the obvious and dramatic volume changes that everyone can recognize after the fact. For example, when you see testing of resistance levels and small corresponding surges in volume, these could be simplified early signs of buying pressure that is about to emerge. The same could hold true for subtle changes in volume accompanying spikes, triangles, and other patterns.

Study volume along with price and seek automated services that provide analyses with moving averages of both features. This information, in combined form, is far more revealing than price changes alone.

Making Charting Valuable— Price and Volume Cycles

The discussions of investing cycles in the market invariably center on price cycles. A stock's pricing might tend to go through growth cycles on a recurring schedule lasting a few months or even several years—to be followed by periods of consolidation or minor correction. So an overall long-term growth pattern is established through price analysis.

It often is just as revealing to track volume cycles, which, while less dependable, also might act as a form of signal concerning the timing of the price cycle. For example, a certain change in volume levels might precede price change movements by a few days or weeks. The problem in tracking volume is the ever-changing nature of the market, particularly the *source* of volume itself. With the popularity and influence of institutional investors (notably mutual funds), it might be impossible to predict long-term trends, or to track the source of trends in the past. The playing field changes constantly.

KEY POINT

A brief study of price and corresponding volume often reveals a relationship, and in some cases changes in price can be anticipated by earlier changes in volume.

Even so, volume changes could signal something. The difficulty for any investor is knowing what such changes are predicting, and whether those changes are positive or negative. You need to track the trends in volume and price, applying the same five rules for all trend analysis, which include the following:

1. *Never consider a single change without analysis of all changes in the past.* Remember the most important rule in trend analysis: Nothing should be reviewed in isolation, and no single movement or change is significant by itself. All material needs to be analyzed in the larger context. Some chartists make the mistake of believing that a single and unconfirmed indication is all that is needed to draw a conclusion. But making an investment decision in haste usually is an expensive choice.

   Every change is only the latest entry in a longer-term trend, whether in business or in personal investing. A stock chart is the representation of a series of changes over time, and all trends are characterized by short-term randomness that can deceive or mislead.

2. *Always use moving averages.* In addition to being cautious about the use of information and avoiding making

KEY POINT

No isolated information has significance except in the way that it adds to the overall trend.

investment decisions based on isolated events, you need to even out the short-term changes shown on a chart. The moving average is a superb tool for the analyst because it helps to avoid the pitfall of overreacting to the latest information and forgetting the purpose of analysis. The moving average evens out the trend by absorbing unusually severe movement. In business, the astute financial analyst knows the importance of viewing sudden and dramatic change with suspicion; the same rule applies to investors.

Moving averages are as important to the chartist as they are to the financial analyst. Because charts are visual tools, it is easy to deceive ourselves into thinking that the latest change is more important than it is. This is similar to the optical illusions we have all seen in which lines appear to be longer than they are because they are attached to arrows pointing outward instead of inward. The stock chart can achieve the same deception when the perception of the analyst is affected by the extent of change. So remember to adhere to the rule that change has to be reviewed within the moving average.

3. *Remember that patterns do not repeat themselves in the same order and with the same timing.* One of the most widely

KEY POINT

Moving averages help us to avoid deceiving ourselves into giving more importance to the latest changes than they deserve.

accepted—and false—beliefs in charting is that patterns are established in both the appearance of the pattern itself and in its timing. In other words, a particular direction in opposition to the established trend is believed to occur in a repetitive way dependably—in terms of shape and scope *and* in terms of timing. So the severity of changes, according to this belief, should be similar from one change to another, and the changes should also occur in a predictable timing pattern.

Both of these beliefs are false. In a review of past price movement, you rarely will see a predictable rhythm to stock price changes. Short-term and intermediate-term charting trends are, indeed, random, even within a predictable trading trend. Avoid falling for the common misconception that the movements in the market are as predictable as the tides. It is an easy belief to accept. We are told that nature acts within the rules of science, that the tides occur with regularity, and so do the seasons. But unlike the tides and the seasons, the market is *not* a product of nature, but of supply and demand. And in regard to predictability, there is nothing natural about the stock market.

KEY POINT

Do not confuse the stock market, or supply and demand, with science or anything else that operates according to natural law.

4. *Consider every possible meaning of a seemingly significant change.* Chartists face the risk that they will draw conclusions too quickly, and that those conclusions will be wrong. In the fast-moving stock market, decisions have to be made quickly or opportunities are lost. Chartists understand the pressure and the need for fast action, and that understanding can lead to a tendency to come to conclusions too quickly.

This is not to suggest that you should ponder a trend for too long, nor that you need to take a lot of time in analysis. You will miss opportunities that way. It does mean that you need to consider all of the possibilities before reaching a conclusion. When you do proceed, it should be with the full knowledge that there may be more than one possible meaning of a change in the trend.

KEY POINT

Investing is particularly interesting when you realize that even the best analysis can be wrong. One of the intriguing points about analysis is that it provides only you with indicators—not sure things.

5. *Remember that "current" information gets old very quickly.* Information in the stock market is by nature fleeting, indeed. Today's fresh news will be stale before this morning's doughnut. The stock market is characterized by the rapid development of information, much of which is dispelled and contradicted, and little of which is of real value. You will find, in fact, that the most valuable information you discover will come from your own hard work. Very little of what you hear "on the street" has any lasting value; most has no value from the moment it is uttered. Wall Street runs on the fuel of rumor, and false information is more plentiful than true information.

KEY POINT

Wall Street believes that information is valuable. But if you look back to yesterday's information, you discover that, in fact, it is pretty cheap—often worthless.

CHAPTER 6

Trends and Averages in Technical Analysis

$\mathbf{A}$ trend is easily identified once underway. The tricky part is recognizing the *next* trend before everyone else.

John Naisbitt says in *Megatrends* that "trends, like horses, are easier to ride in the direction they are already going." The observation is accurate. It is easy to see a trend that is underway. The purpose of analyzing trends using technical indicators is not to recognize what is already visible, but to anticipate what is about to happen.

Trends occur in all markets. Whether you follow fundamental or technical indicators, or a combination of both, certain trends can be recognized and used to your advantage. If you can accurately estimate the upcoming changes in trends, you have a heads up before everyone else—because the overall general tendency in the market is to follow, not to lead. You need to

KEY POINT

Trends are not interesting for historical purposes, even though they are historically based. It is what they tell us about the future that is really interesting.

acknowledge that trends occur for often irrational reasons, and your real advantage comes from seeing what is about to happen, not from understanding why. For example, when the overall mood of the market is turning pessimistic, it does not necessarily matter that a particular company is experiencing spectacular profits and growth. It might be dragged down with the larger market mood as reflected in the Dow Jones Industrial Average (DJIA) and other indexes.

KEY POINT

Trends have as much to do with the market mood as with hard facts—often more.

If your personal technical analysis system includes trend analysis of a simplified and manageable nature, you will need to develop not only the tracking mechanisms, but the discipline to watch your indicators carefully and keep them up to date. A trend that is not watched has no value.

The Key to Success in Technical Analysis— Tracking for Prediction

In Chapter 5, the common charting patterns for prices were summarized. Recognition of these patterns is not, by itself, a valuable tool because mere recognition tells you nothing about the future of that stock. The real value comes when the pattern tells you what is likely to occur next.

With practice, you will be able to skillfully interpret a chart as patterns emerge—not with absolute accuracy because no such forecasting tool exists, but with a degree of expertise that can work to confirm other indicators. Some examples follow.

Primary Cycle Movements

A broad view of a stock's trading pattern might reveal a classic primary cycle movement. This is the three-stage process illustrated in Figure 5.4. The first movement represents a generalized trend up or down, the second is a plateau effect, and the third is a generalized trend opposite of the first direction. Because this movement is long-term, the important question is, "How do I recognize when you are at or near the conclusion of one of the three steps?" Of course, you cannot. However, if you want to invest in a stock for the long term, a study of recent months and years and a recognition of a long-term primary cycle movement can act as a helpful tool in the timing of your investment.

If the stock appears to have undergone a lengthy downward trend and has flattened out over recent months, it may rise if the primary cycle movement pattern is followed. It is all a matter of timing as to when you should invest. And of course, this observation should come as confirming information to other, independent analyses.

The opposite argument can be made for the reverse primary cycle movement. If the stock in question shows a primary cycle movement in the past and has risen and then gone to the second stage plateau, this could act as an indicator that a likely third phase will be bearish.

KEY POINT

All changes, even the clearest seeming ones, should be confirmed by different and independent indicators.

Head and Shoulders

The classic head and shoulders pattern can serve as a useful form of confirmation for other signs and trend reversals because it is a representation of what occurs in patterns of support and resistance. The head and shoulders pattern cannot be depended on to act as a repetitive pattern. But the peak of a head and shoulders pattern indicates the location of a resistance level, just as an inverse head and shoulders identifies support.

Some chartists like to think of the head and shoulders pattern as a primary indicator, to be confirmed by other information. However, the pattern works primarily to confirm primary movements. It is the repetitive sign found in head and shoulders that makes it so valuable for confirmation purposes. The shoulder peaks with the head in between represent a form of repetitive indication that indicates reversals of previously established trends. Because every previous trend reverses itself at some point, the head and shoulders is usually a strong sign that reversal is imminent—but only as a confirming indicator, and never by itself.

No matter how reliable an indicator, and no matter how significant it appears to be, the same general rule of trend analysis must be applied: Nothing is taken as an indicator by itself, in isolation from other information. Every indicator is part of a larger process in trend analysis. The head and shoulders pattern is a fine visual representation of changes—subtle or obvious—in the prevailing supply and demand circumstances. Those cycles are changing constantly, and head and shoulders tells you that change in the pattern is about to occur—again, assuming that other indicators support this conclusion as well.

KEY POINT

The head and shoulders pattern is a classic example of how support and resistance work in price patterns.

Support and Resistance

Perhaps the most important concept in technical analysis is that of support and resistance. A stock's trading pattern might appear random in the day-to-day changes of price and ranges of trading activity. But support and resistance can be used to assess volatility and to identify and anticipate change, perhaps with greater dependability than any other technical or short-term indicator.

The auction marketplace is a reflection of interaction between buyers and sellers. As a general rule, when prices fall, the stock is more attractive and the resultant buying activity drives the price upward, which in turn makes the stock less attractive. And so the interaction goes on and on. In such a market, there is no random pattern to stock trading. All price movement reflects current attitudes among buyers and sellers. Thus, support and resistance are important defining tools for every analyst.

Support is the bottom price at which a seller is willing to sell and a buyer is willing to buy. But the identification of this level, by itself, has no meaning. Support becomes important in two respects. First, it helps you to identify the degree of risk or potential at any given price. The support level, if it appears solid, defines the likely current risk level in that stock. If you believe the stock is not likely to fall below the current support level in the near future, then downside risk is limited. The second value of support analysis comes if and when the price begins to test its support level, perhaps falling below that level in the trading range over several days and finally breaking through altogether. These trends can be recognized as they develop.

Resistance is somewhat different. Like support, resistance is a defining level. It represents the highest price level at which buyers are willing to pay and the highest level at which it is possible for sellers to sell the stock. The resistance level is important as an indication about the timing of purchases. For example, if you are tracking a particular stock and thinking of buying it, a study of resistance level and the trading pattern could indicate when the price might break through. As resistance levels are tested over a period of days, a breakthrough could be anticipated.

Charting offers a nice analytical advantage because it is visual. The support and resistance levels of a stock, reviewed over time, indicate long-term cycles for the stock. In charting as elsewhere, a lot of emphasis is placed on upward and downward trends. Some

less patient investors find themselves frustrated when their investments move within a narrow trading band and do not provide them
the excitement of volatile upward or downward movement.

A lack of broader price movement within a given time frame
might indicate low volatility in the stock, or it might also be a
sign that trading has taken a breather. In the supply and demand
cycle, periods of rapid change might be followed by offsetting
periods of relative inaction. So support and resistance can be used
not only to spot breakouts from a previous narrow trading range;
they also can be used to observe and evaluate the meaning of the
trading range itself. The stock that is at rest in terms of trading
interest is not necessarily an uninteresting prospect; at times, the
stocks with fewer active indicators might seem dormant for very
interesting reasons. If you are able to spot a trend related to support and resistance in a relatively narrow range, you might also
gain some market advantage. Support and resistance are more
than confirming indicators at times, and might serve as timing
mechanisms themselves.

A study of support and resistance together might further
define the volatility—or market risk—of a stock. Obviously, a
very narrow trading range that stays within support and resistance levels over many months reveals little. And any apparent
testing of support and resistance might not be significant by
itself, making it difficult to anticipate change. And if change
does occur, it might not be very broad. Double top and double
bottom formations without breakthrough serve as indicators
that, rather than breaking through a support or resistance level,
a stock price is likely to head in the opposite direction. Thus, a
double top without successful breakthrough above resistance

KEY POINT

Support and resistance are the basic concepts in
charting. They serve as a sign, by way of patterns and
changes in those patterns, of a stock's volatility and risk.

could foretell a bearish trend, and a double bottom without successful breakthrough below support could foretell a bullish trend.

The Broadening Formation

The megaphone-shaped broadening formation is one in which support and resistance are both expanding. This information is troubling to the risk-sensitive investor because you cannot know which direction the stock will move if, indeed, it does break out. In effect, the broadening formation is a concurrent breakthrough of both support and resistance. This growing volatility, especially if sudden, could mean many things, but without independent indications about whether the trend is positive or negative, the broadening formation is difficult to read.

KEY POINT

Broadening formations are troubling because they are ambiguous, whereas the classical support and resistance patterns show more clearly what is going on. Unfortunately, price patterns do not always conform to the theories about them.

Triangles

The opposite pattern, a narrowing trading range, represents a reduction in volatility, which might be a positive signal, an indication that the stock's tendencies are quieting down. But triangles are difficult to interpret as they are developing, notably if they occur in a series of sudden bursts of volatility followed by triangular patterning. You might learn more from the triangle by studying which side—support or resistance—moves the least. If support is stronger than resistance—meaning, it changes less—this is a sign that price support is strong even though trading range is narrowing. If resistance tends to be flatter than support, this is a sign of subtle but consistent strengthening in two respects: First, the range is narrowing in an upward trend in the short term and, second, the volatility factor is decreasing at the same time.

KEY POINT

Triangles are used to analyze subtle changes in support and resistance, and to recognize or confirm changing trends.

Flags and Pennants

The flags and pennants pattern might occur in rapid succession and might have special significance or no meaning whatsoever. It is important when studying such patterns also to have independent confirmation of your conclusions, as flags and pennants by themselves do not give you enough information to act. These are the kinds of patterns created by interim movement of stock prices, and they might not have special significance. This makes the flags and pennants formation troubling. You cannot know with any reliability whether it signifies anything.

KEY POINT

Flags and pennants occur in short-term trading activity, but the real significance of the pattern can be established only by studying interim patterns over a long period of time. Different stocks show different flags and pennants patterns.

Wedges

A wedge, like a triangle, is a narrowing price range. An important distinction, though, is that the wedge appears in one of two forms. A wedge whose resistance level remains fairly consistent while its support level rises signifies a downside breakthrough (as shown in Figure 5.13 in the last chapter). A wedge whose support level remains consistent while the price range is narrowing might end with a positive-trend breakthrough.

> **KEY POINT**
>
> Wedges are narrowing formations that also demonstrate whether support or resistance is holding—and this can work as an early signal of change in a trend.

Gaps

The gap comes in several classifications and can provide useful information in technical analysis. A gap is significant because it is created by a space between one day's trading range and that of the next. In the common trend of stock prices, a trading range will overlap from one day to the next. Gaps indicate that something unusual is occurring and should be heeded with that in mind. When gaps occur in the trading range, also check volume to see if any sudden changes are taking place there as well. The gap could signify and forecast changes in trends of price movement speed or direction. The gap, by itself, should be a sign that you need to watch the stock carefully. But of greater interest still are the various types of gap formation. These may occur when dramatic changes are taking place in the stock's price.

> **KEY POINT**
>
> A gap in a stock's trading range could have significance, especially if a series of repetitive gaps occurs in a short period of time.

Spikes

A spike is high or low point in the trading range of the stock. Pay attention to the significance of head and shoulders patterns, which occur at times with the triple spike effect—two shoulders on either end of the head, or spike. The spike might have important significance as the top-most point in an upward trend, or as the bottom-most point of a downward trend. This is one of those patterns that is spotted easily in hindsight, but is difficult to judge as it is happening. Some stocks, however, go through spiking patterns as they move through their cycles, and you can begin to recognize those patterns and time your buy and sell decisions accordingly.

KEY POINT

A spike is most interesting when it is compared to what occurred just before the spike, and to what occurs right afterward.

Reversal Days

A final element of price patterns is the *reversal day*, which is the point at which a stock's pattern changes direction. Often accompanied by a spike or the more moderate head and shoulders pattern, the reversal day is recognized on the upside when a stock

KEY POINT

It is, perhaps, the essence of technical analysis to be able to recognize price reversals. The reversal day—when prices change directions—is the key to this recognition requirement.

closes below the previous day's close, or on the downside when a stock closes above the previous day's close. This is not a hard-and-fast rule, but merely an observation of a common pattern in trading.

Developing an Efficient Trend Approach

Of course, your hindsight is always better. The purpose in going through the common patterns and describing their possible significance is to demonstrate that, with some practice, you can develop a sense of the rhythm of a particular stock. That is the key point to be made. No two stocks have identical patterns or timing, and even a particular issue is likely to move through cycles with entirely dissimilar patterns from one period to the next. It is critical to remember that corporations are vibrant, competitive, and dynamic. They change all of the time as they move into markets aggressively, retreat on discovery of mistakes, retrench, attack in other markets, expand, take on new product lines, acquire smaller companies, and do all of the other things that companies do. The common theme is growth and change.

KEY POINT

Not only is the stock market ever-changing, the patterns of change are never the same. This makes the process of investing risky, potentially profitable, and very, very interesting.

In such an environment, you cannot expect a company's stock to repeat patterns with any dependability. Ironically, it is this very lack of dependability in trading patterns that identifies the most promising stock market investments: those companies that are in growth mode. Once a company settles down for its acceptable fatness and stops trying, it no longer can be called a growth stock, and it should be taken off the list. You should want ever-changing corporations as investments, companies whose stock price patterns reflect the ever-growing and ever-improving nature of the companies themselves. The chaos and excitement of growth and competition are reflected in the stock price pattern—chaotic, unpredictable, and subject to sudden and unexplainable price swings. Even when those price swings cannot be specifically explained, much less predicted, the patterns themselves are what make growth stocks the most viable.

With this in mind, you must ask yourself, "How can I possibly develop an efficient trend analysis strategy?" It is a good question. Because the companies with the greatest potential as investments should be unpredictable (you would expect as much in an environment of change), you also cannot expect cycles to repeat last year's patterns. Essentially, the growing company is forever reinventing itself, so that this year it is an entirely different organization than it was last year.

The answer to the question, of course, is that you cannot expect dependable or reliable means for anticipating short-term price change. But you can come up with a system that gives you something even more valuable: a means for recognizing the patterns in a stock's price that are likely to signify the near-term direction in price and price range. This is the purpose of charting—to be able to understand how a particular phenomenon in a trading pattern is likely to lead to the next phase. There is no guarantee, only a likelihood. And in the stock market, that is the best you can expect.

KEY POINT

The purpose in charting is not to know what prices will do next, as some believe; rather, it is to be able to identify likely patterns of change based on price movement.

To develop a dependable program of trend analysis, you will need to achieve the following.

Timely Capturing of Information

The first step is to have the means for getting the information you need on a timely basis. If you have access to the Internet, stock quotes are widely available, so there is no problem getting closing prices. You also need chart resources to get trading ranges and volume for each day. If you do not have Internet access, you need to be in touch with a brokerage service so that you can retrieve the daily information you need.

KEY POINT

Timeliness of information is absolutely essential. Old data—even if accurate—gives you nothing of any value in estimating the short-term future.

Method for Visual Summation

The second step is to develop a way to summarize the information in a charted format that is useful to you. Again, if you are on the Internet, the work is done for you already and simply can be viewed out of your "favorites" folder once you decide which service to use. Many include daily trading ranges and closing prices as well as a moving average.

KEY POINT

One way to ensure that your data is invalid is to gather too much of it. Make sure that you collect only what you need and that you put it to good use.

Method for Interpretation

The third critical step is to understand what the information means. Many investors forget to take this all-important step and are satisfied with the possession of timely information, which is only the first step. That information is useful only if you are able to use it to develop a strategy, to understand what significant changes in trends are taking place (or better yet, about to take place), and to understand what those changes mean to you in terms of risk or potential reward. The stock owner needs to watch out for risk in order to time the selling of shares, and the stock watcher needs to look for potential reward in order to time purchases.

KEY POINT

Remember that having valuable information in hand is not enough. You also need to know what it means and how to react—these are the essential requirements for successful investing.

Decision Point

The final step is to take action. If you are tracking a stock, you need to buy at what seems the best possible moment. If you own

KEY POINT

A common failure is to rely too heavily on the gathering of information and on analysis. While buried deeply in mathematical equations and thinking about the likely future outcome of price patterns, you could miss important opportunities. Successful investors act quickly and decisively.

stock, you must decide whether to buy more, hold, or sell. You need to include in your program this essential fourth step, or the entire exercise will be just that—an exercise. All of the other steps are there specifically in support of your decision step.

Using Charting as a Tracking Tool

Free charting resources are widely available on the Internet, meaning that you do not need to go through any of the time-consuming steps of finding information and placing it on a chart, or calculating ever-changing moving averages. The resources below are only a sampling of what is available as of March, 1999. You might discover other resources by performing a further search.

ASK Research	www.askresearch.com/cgi-bin/chart
BigCharts	www.bigcharts.com
INVESTools Charting	www.investools.com/cgi-bin/charts.pl?
StockMaster	www.stockmaster.com
StockSite	www.stocksite.com/research
timely.com	www.timely.com
Wall Street City	www.wallstreetcity.com/leaders/stocks_y.asp
justquotes.com	www.webfn.com

Tracking Volume

Many of the resources above will allow you to track price *and* volume for your stocks or for stocks you are tracking with the possibility of investing in the future. Volume is critically important in the charting of stocks, because it often tells you *why* a stock's price trend is changing, or at least provides indications that some form of change is about to occur.

Not only can volume act as a warning sign or heads-up of emerging trends in price, but it also can be a confirming factor. Most of all, volume often leads the price trend, so growth in the interest in a stock is likely to show up in increased volume before it is reflected in price. This is true with buying interest as well as selling interest. In this respect, the word *interest* refers to both, an interest in buying shares and an interest in selling shares.

KEY POINT

The fact that trends in volume often signal changes in price beforehand makes volume tracking essential to the technician.

Obviously, heavy volume accompanying rising prices is bullish on the surface of the trend, and heavy volume with downside price movement is bearish. But the more interesting observation for the technician is that, indeed, the volume trend does lead the price trend.

Heavy volume tends to precede significant price movement by weeks or even months; so your observation of changes in volume levels can serve as perhaps a better indicator of future price changes than price charting itself. Volume also indicates when price trends are beginning to exhaust themselves. As primary trends begin reaching their top (in bull markets) or bottom (in bear markets), the corresponding level of volume tends to drop off well ahead of the price change, serving as an early warning signal. If you have been buying in a rising market, a slackening in volume could act as a hold signal—to be followed by a sale as prices begin leveling off. Again, this is all a matter of timing and, at least partially, of luck. On the downside, if you have left the market and are tracking a bear tendency, watch volume as well. As selling activity begins slowing, so will downside volume. In fact, high levels of downside volume might well be replaced by activity in buying pressure, resulting in higher volume levels brought about by buyers (rather than by sellers)—a sign that many investors now perceive that the market contains many bargains at current prices. That would be a bottom in the trend.

The measurement of volume requires an analysis of upside versus downside volume. Remember, it is not enough to know how many shares trade in a day, week, or month in a particular stock. It is of far greater significance to know the source of that volume—buyers or sellers.

> ### KEY POINT
>
> Technical analysis of volume requires knowing more than just the number of shares traded. You also need to know whether volume is created by buyers or by sellers.

The *upside/downside volume line* compares the volume in stocks rising in value with the volume of stocks falling in value. As a broad indicator, this is a useful tool because it shows where the weight of activity is occurring over a large sample, namely the entire market. It would be impossible to quantify volume as strictly bull or bear, remembering that every trade has a buyer and a seller. However, the upside/downside comparison shows which stocks—those rising or those falling—are dominant. When studied over a period of time, the trend is revealing about the overall market, especially as the degree of favor toward upside or downside remains or increases.

The upside/downside analysis of volume should track the same trends in prices overall. That is to say, if volume consistently

> ### KEY POINT
>
> It is important to know the difference between upside volume and downside volume—assuming that stock prices will follow the trading activity reflected in volume levels.

shows a pattern of upside trend over downside trend, then the prices of stocks (again, overall) should show the same tendency. To the extent that the volume trend precedes the price trend, volume tracking can indicate when the current price trend is about to change.

A long-term study of volume using moving averages over a period of months and years will reveal that the average trend in volume precedes that of price and signals major turns away from current price trends. This can be valuable information. In the modern environment where controls automatically can suspend trading, and where electronic communication makes trading convenient and instantaneous, long-term comparisons are not valid. Not only has the trend in upside/downside volume only been in existence since 1965, but the way the market works has changed drastically in recent years. This means that the reporting and tracking of volume, even if truly valid and comparable, cannot take into account the factor of electronic trading. Today, more volume on the market is managed more efficiently than in the past when trading was done in person or by telephone and computers were nonexistent or terribly slow.

KEY POINT

A study of long-term volume has to take into account the greater speed, efficiency, and transaction methods in use today versus the slower systems of the past. Older systems would not have been able to handle today's volume levels.

Volume analysis should be performed with these limitations in mind, and only with a forward-looking mentality. Too much history can distort your long-term averages because the methods of trading—and overall volume itself—have changed so drastically. As with all trend analysis, it is critical to ensure that the entire range and scope of the period studied is of like value. At many times in the past, anxious would-be sellers or buyers were forced to wait a day, and sometimes longer, during heavy-volume periods, simply because they could not get through on the telephone to their broker.

A pattern of advancing versus declining issues based on volume is a fine indicator of overall trends, and also might signal major price trend changes. Another method of studying this relationship is to track what is called the *breadth advance/ decline indicator*. This is a study comparing the total number of advancing issues to the total number of declining issues. When studied in connection with a trend, this shorthand version of volume analysis is helpful in determining exactly what kinds of tendencies—bull or bear—are underway, and what kind of staying power they contain.

The breadth index is usually calculated on New York Stock Exchange (NYSE) issues using the following three steps:

1. Calculate the average of the number of advancing issues from the past ten days.
2. Calculate the average of the number of declining issues from the past ten days.
3. Divide the ten-day average of advancing issues by the sum of the average of advancing issues and the average of declining issues. The result is expressed as a factor, with 1.00 being a completely neutral response. Anything above zero is bullish, and anything below is bearish (remembering, of course, that each calculation represents the latest entry in a longer-term trend).

Example: In one sector, a study of 250 stocks shows the following: the average of the past ten days was 145 advances and 105 declines. The advance/decline calculation is:

$$\frac{145}{145 + 105} \quad = \quad 0.58$$

The full formula for calculation of the breadth advance/decline indicator is:

$$\frac{(A1 \ldots A10) \div 10}{(A1 \ldots A10 + D1 \ldots D10) \div 10} = B$$

$$
\begin{aligned}
A &= \text{advancing issues} \\
D &= \text{declining issues} \\
B &= \text{breadth index} \\
1 \ldots 10 &= \text{days in the moving average}
\end{aligned}
$$

The moving average almost always is recommended in calculations of this sort because it evens out temporary aberrations and makes your analysis easier. You can perform a week-long form of the same study using sums for the entire week if you do not wish to calculate the average; however, the average is computed easily in very little time and provides you with useful and valuable information.

Studying the Volatility of Stocks

The study of a stock's volatility is perhaps as important as the study of support and resistance. *Volatility* is the relative degree of tendency a stock's price demonstrates to swing between a range of high-to-low prices. Volatility is an indication of market risk. The more volatile a stock's tendency, the greater the market risk. And remembering that risk and potential for growth are related directly; the more volatile stocks will offer the greater potential for near-term growth in value.

Volatility in terms of price is measured most readily by comparing the current price to the price range. Most stock listings provide you the information you need to perform this calculation. You need the 52-week high and low prices (the range) to

KEY POINT

Volatility is often overlooked in the analysis of stocks, but it is a key indicator of risk and growth potential.

calculate volatility. Stocks also might show trends toward increasing or decreasing volatility. This will show up on a price chart as well as in a volatility study.

To calculate, first compute the difference in price between the 52-week high and low, and then divide this by the annual low. The result, expressed as a percentage, provides you the means for comparisons of volatility between different stocks. This is the formula for volatility:

$$\frac{\text{annual high} - \text{annual low}}{\text{annual low}} \quad = \quad \text{volatility \%}$$

Example: A stock's 52-week price range shows the high/low at 38/27. Volatility is calculated by dividing the difference by the low:

$$\frac{38 - 27}{27} \quad = \quad 40.7\%$$

Another stock's high/low is 58/55. Its volatility is:

$$\frac{58 - 55}{55} \quad = \quad 5.5\%$$

These two examples demonstrate how volatility differs between stocks. In the first example, the trading range is 11 points and volatility is 40.7 percent; in the second, the trading range is only 3 points and volatility is 5.5 percent.

Odd Lot Trading Trends

Another interesting indicator to watch that signals changes in technical trends is the *odd lot short indicator*. This is a widely followed indicator that is based on trends among odd lot traders. As a general rule, investors trade in *round lots* of 100 shares or more, while institutions trade in blocks of 1,000, 5,000, and 10,000 shares. But the most inexperienced investors often will trade in what are called *odd lots*, or lots of stock of fewer than 100 shares. So the odd lot theory is based on the

> **KEY POINT**
>
> The study of odd lot short selling is based on the premise that odd lot traders are usually wrong. Ironically, the *majority* of traders are usually wrong, not just odd lot traders.

belief that odd lot traders are usually wrong in their judgments about the market.

The indicator is based on a study of selling by odd lot traders in comparison with trends in the overall market. When odd lot short selling volume is high relative to the rest of the market—meaning that odd lot sellers expect the market to fall—it is taken as an indication that the market is at the bottom and will rise. And by the opposite reasoning, when odd lot selling volume is low relative to the rest of the market, it is taken as a sign that the market is at the top, and is about to fall. As long as the odd lot short-selling trends are always wrong, then one would do the exact opposite of the odd lot short seller.

This type of study works as a method of comparing price and volume together. Price, of course, affects conditions that cause odd lot sellers to act in a particular manner, so odd lot short sales reflect price changes. At the same time, the volume of trading activity is measured in a relative fashion—odd lot trends versus overall market trends—so that both price and volume have important roles in such a study.

> **KEY POINT**
>
> Odd lot short sale trading patterns are reflections of both price and volume and reaction to it. But in today's market, odd lot traders cannot be written off as entirely wrong, because the market and methods of investing have both changed drastically.

You can measure odd lot trends in a number of ways; the objective is to track the current trend, looking for changes in sentiment. The odd lot short activity should be compared to overall market short selling, with the ratio expressed as a percentage. Another method is to compare short-selling activity to buying activity. On the overall market, a ratio can be developed to show the overall trend. This, compared to the same ratio calculated for odd lot traders alone, will provide the means for comparison that you need. According to this theory, as the odd lot ratio grows higher than the overall market, or falls lower, the current trend changes.

Price-Earnings Ratio as a Hybrid Analytical Device

The price-earnings ratio, or *PE*, is perhaps the most interesting of all analytical tools for two reasons. First, it is a hybrid combining fundamental (earnings) with technical (price) data to arrive at a "factor" that defines the investment value or viability of a stock. Second, as a matter of history, investors consistently misread the PE.

Computed by dividing the current market price by earnings, PE should be more controversial than it is because of the perception in the market about what it means, which is often wrong. Investors generally believe that exceptionally low PE stocks have little future potential for growth, and that relatively high PE stocks have exceptional growth value. The outcome of long-term studies, however, demonstrates that lower-than-average PE stocks consistently out-perform higher-than-average PE stocks.[*]

What does this mean? We can assume that investors generally tend to underestimate the growth potential of stocks that appear unexciting or lackluster (as reflected in a lower-than-average PE)

---

[*]Sanjoy Basu's 14-month study of 500 New York Stock Exchange issues, 1977, and David Dremen's 9-year study of 1,200 stocks between 1968 and 1977, which showed lower PE stocks yielding an average of 7.89 percent and higher-than-average PE stocks yielding only 0.33 percent.

KEY POINT

Even with long-term evidence that opinions about PE levels are wrong, investors continue to track the PE—and to draw the wrong conclusions about it.

and, even more significant, that they also tend to overestimate the future potential of today's big movers and shakers in the market (as reflected in a higher-than-average PE).

This information can be used to identify levels of risk and potential growth, not in traditional ways followed by the majority, but with insight about the historical studies that show how wrong the majority of investors are much of the time. PE is a good measure of market risk. It can help you to understand relative risk levels of otherwise similar stocks just by comparing their PE ratios. For example, if you consider a PE range between 11 and 20 to be "normal" in terms of risk evaluation, then you also will understand the potential risk/reward of stocks falling above and below that range.

You need to ensure, however, that your comparison is performed on a valid basis. The PE changes each day as a result of ever-changing prices, but the earnings factor is historically set. As the length of time since the latest earnings report increases, the PE grows ever more inaccurate. For example, if a company's earnings report came out only one week ago, the current PE is a pretty reliable indicator about how price and earnings are related. But if a comparable company's latest earnings report

KEY POINT

The current PE is inaccurate if the earnings report is outdated, a critical point often ignored completely.

is nearly three months old, its current PE is more questionable. Based on what the next earnings report shows, the level of a new PE might be vastly different from the level at which it is reported today.

Be aware as you compare PEs that the time since the latest earnings report is an important qualifying factor. It would add to the accuracy of investors' analytical processes if the financial press could encode the PE to indicate the age of the current earnings report with this problem in mind. However, even if it were possible to have a fully updated PE for every company, you would also need to be aware of the potential for manipulation of profit levels by corporate management. The accounting rules allow so much latitude to management and to auditing firms that it is possible to create the appearance of more consistency than an accurate report would show. This is allowed to continue within the guidelines because stockholders prefer consistency in profits and dividends *and* long-term growth of their investments. If it requires a few minor adjustments in the timing and reporting of transactions, it is not considered a large problem.

The PE should be included in virtually all forms of analysis, whether you favor the technical or the fundamental. Most investors use it as a method of evaluating potential for growth in the price of the stock; however, its real value is in the stock-to-stock comparisons it provides in risk evaluation. Its utility for judging potential for growth is only as a secondary value. You also can use PE for tracking the changes in your portfolio in terms of perception about the company. Once you have shares of a stock in your portfolio, changes in the PE reflect investors' overall impressions of the company by indicating their reaction, represented in market price, to changes in the company's earnings. While many other factors affect price, the earnings reports cannot be ignored as one of the most important factors.

As valuable and universally accepted as PE is as an analytical tool, it can be unreliable as well. Stock market people like fresh information, and they like to revise and update frequently. With this in mind, the PE is an odd tool for analysis because the information going into it can be quite old. Oddly enough, it usually is a reflection of some very new information (price) and some very old information (earnings).

Remember what the PE is—a comparison between the current stock price per share and the most recently published earnings per share. Because we know on a daily basis the current price of a stock, that side of the ratio is always current. However, earnings reports come out only quarterly, so the earnings side of the PE could be as old as 90 days. So the longer the period since the last-issued financial report, the less reliable the PE.

Making the problem even more complex is the way in which interim earnings reports are prepared. The full-blown annual report is the result of an extensive and detailed independent audit. The auditing firm checks transactions and accounting decisions made during the year and ensures that all proper conventions have been followed. By the time the final audited statement is released, the company's books and records have been reviewed with a fine-toothed comb, and any required adjustments have been made. In spite of the wide latitude given in accounting and auditing principles, the audited financial statement can be reasonably relied upon to accurately reflect the year's earnings.

The same is not true of quarterly reports. While the books might be reviewed by an independent auditing firm, the degree of auditing and examination is far less than for the annual report. So the three mid-year financial reports are not as reliable in terms of the accuracy of earnings. A PE based on earnings per share 10 or 11 months into a corporation's fiscal year could be highly inaccurate.

With this in mind, it is troubling that few people seem concerned with the problem. It seems that virtually no one asks the important questions about the PE, like "When did the fiscal year end?" or "When was the last quarterly report?" Obviously, a PE in the early months of the fiscal year is going to be far more accurate and reliable than one in the final few months.

It could be surmised that, because all corporations are audited in a similar manner, they all have relatively identical problems in reliability. But that is a poor argument. Inaccurate information is unacceptable, even when everyone has the same level of inaccuracy. What you need is reliable information. Because the PE problem is so widespread, it is advisable to continue using it only as a benchmark for overall impression, and to depend on more current information for the big decisions. The PE certainly should be included in your analytical arsenal, but in cases where the PE contradicts other, more recent indicators, it should be discounted— especially if the latest annual report is not very recent.

CHAPTER 7

Valuable Indicators You Can Use

Investment analysts always have enjoyed mathematical study of the market, even before the days of computerization. The analyst works with models and attempts to demonstrate that those models show a degree of order within the market. Unfortunately, the market is a significantly disordered place. It is driven not so much by precise formulas, but by the whims of the public, supply and demand, invisible cyclical factors, and the unknown. With this in mind, we need to recognize that indicators can be placed into three broad groups, based on users of those indicators.

The first group is the purely academic. Analysis developed in academic environments often involves very abstract concepts about the economics of the market and is difficult for most

KEY POINT

Academic analysis is useful in school, where professors might be confident about what their analysis means. But you always should ask how much money they have invested.

153

ordinary folks to comprehend. Even more to the point, purely academic indicators are of no value to investors. Some fine market studies have come from academic research and analysis of historical price and volume movement that was conducted in an attempt to prove a theory, but those studies do not help you to determine how, when, or where you should invest your money.

The second group is the practical but highly technical indicator. The technician who studies the market for a living and makes recommendations based on detailed analysis and the development of models has a specific need for information and uses that information in a very specialized way. For most investors, the highly technical form of analysis is not worth the time it would take to master it, even though the results can be very useful. Some of these results are available from brokerage houses or subscription services.

KEY POINT

Many professionals develop models for the detailed and intricate study of some phase of the market, but those models do not really help you decide when to buy, hold, or sell.

The third group is the type of indicator that everyone can use. This group is not too technical and the concepts are easily grasped. The formulas also are easy to compute so that you can develop your own trend analysis and moving average. This is the group of indicators that are included in this chapter. We offer only a few of the more useful indicators, rather than attempt to produce a broader array of detailed indicators, many of which would not be useful in putting together a program of your own.

Indicators dealing with price and price movement may help confirm chart patterns or independent fundamental information you derive from other sources. Volume indicators help you to anticipate price movement of specific stocks.

KEY POINT

The truly valuable indicator is the one that gives you information—not definitive answers, just more information—that you can incorporate into your own program.

Popular Technical Formulas

The Insider Buy and Sell

One of the most useful price indicators is the *insider buy or sell*. An insider is anyone in a position to know more than the general public about a company and its stock. Insiders include officers, members of the board of directors, or owners of large amounts of stock. If a company's stock is traded publicly, all insider trades are registered with the Securities and Exchange Commission each month.

Because insiders do have more knowledge than the investing public, they are forbidden to profit from their knowledge. Because they are insiders, however, their particular trading in the company stock is of considerable interest to outsiders, or the investing public. The insider knows about upcoming acquisitions, mergers, and new product lines, and has an understanding of the fair market price of the stock. So when the price falls to bargain levels, an insider knows it is time to buy.

Investors track insider activity through the financial press or subscription services such as ValueLine. You can develop a system of your own that is especially suited to your own opinion about this indicator. You might simply keep track of the

KEY POINT

Insider transactions are worth watching because the people making the trades are closest to the action.

number of insider trades, watching to see whether they buy or sell. Remembering that insiders might enter into transactions as part of a regular investment program or for personal reasons not significant or meaningful to future price changes, it is still useful to track the trend in insider trades. For example, if many insider trades occur (on the buy or sell side) after a period of relative quiet, that certainly is worth investigation. The insider trend is a valuable signal that might not tell the whole story by itself, but that could lead you to other indicators in a search for confirmation.

The Mutual Funds Cash/Assets Ratio

One group of investors that has an exceptionally large influence on the market is the mutual fund. Hundreds of funds invest billions of dollars and, like insiders, the management of these funds might be well connected with the management of the major companies whose stock they hold. Thus, the activity of trading within a large mutual fund can have a lot to do with how that stock fares with other investors. In other words, if a mutual fund (or several funds) buys up shares in a particular company, it creates a scarcity of available shares, driving up the market price. And when funds begin selling large amounts of holdings, it creates a glut in the market and leads to weakness in price. In this respect, mutual funds have great influence on the market price of stocks beyond the pure supply and demand cycle.

KEY POINT

Mutual funds account for such a large percentage of total market volume that they have great influence on price. It is important, though, to note that mutual fund decisions are wrong more often than they are right.

The *mutual funds cash/assets ratio* shows changes in the trend among large institutional investors to invest capital or to hold out until changes occur in the market. The formula for the mutual funds cash/assets ratio is:

$$\frac{\text{cash}}{\text{total assets}} = \text{ratio}$$

Generally speaking, it is thought to be a bad sign when a mutual fund has relatively little uninvested cash relative to its total assets, and when the ratio is relatively high, it is a positive sign. This is a contrary indicator, based on the belief that fund management usually is wrong—a belief borne out by the history of mutual fund market performance.*

Mutual funds have great influence over the market, and a study of trends among them always provides a useful insight into the overall trends. A Web site of great value in collecting statistics about individual funds as well as the overall market is the Investment Company Institute site (www.ici.org). This site provides many useful forms of information and statistics, including the latest information about rates of return, fees and charges, and free articles about funds.

The New High/New Low Ratio

Another useful form of analysis is that of new highs and new lows. When a stock reaches new high or low levels within a 52-week period, the change is always significant for the company involved. And when an overall market trend shows significant change in high or low levels overall, it has importance for the market as a whole.

---

*A recent study of mutual fund performance showed that only 10 percent of all funds exceeded the market average when compared to the Standard & Poor's 500. A January 11, 1998, article in the *New York Times* cited a survey by Morningstar, Inc., that reported the following dismal results among diversified stock funds: in 1994, only 24 percent of funds beat the market; in 1995, 16 percent; in 1996, 26 percent; and in 1997, only 10 percent beat market averages.

To compute the *new high/new low ratio*, divide the new highs by the new lows and report the outcome in the form of a percentage. The formula for this ratio is:

$$\frac{\text{number of new high issues}}{\text{number of new low issues}} = \text{ratio}$$

The number of new high and new low issues is reported daily in the financial press, and is almost universally recognized as an important technical signal. As with all indicators, you should use a moving average to discover a trend. As the number of new high issues grows, it is considered a bullish sign for future price levels for the market overall, and the change will be reflected in a growing percentage outcome in the ratio. And if the number of new lows grows relative to new highs, it is seen as a negative indicator for future price levels.

KEY POINT

New high/new low analysis is a reliable indicator of market sentiment because it efficiently reflects record-setting price levels for the overall market. It is a broad measurement of a trend.

Interestingly, the new high/new low ratio, because it deals with a full year of analysis in a moving average, actually serves as a longer-term indicator than most technical indicators. It provides a statistical base for anticipating future price directions as far out as a year. Significant changes in this ratio indicate the general intermediate-term direction of the market.

The importance of studying the entire market and using a moving average cannot be emphasized too much. In this indicator, we merely count the number of stocks reaching historical high and low levels. This does not take into consideration some important qualifying facts, such as extraordinary or exceptional financial news, mergers and acquisitions, the size and influence of the companies in the mix, or any other factors; it is merely a count of stocks reaching new record levels when compared to the past 52 weeks.

Advance/Decline Studies

A related study involves the analysis of the number of issues advancing and the number of issues declining; in other words, the number of stocks whose market value went up and the number whose value went down. These statistics are available every day in the financial press.

The number of advancing issues as well as the number of declining issues should be studied in a moving average. You may use daily numbers or weekly totals, but in either case apply a moving average in order to study the trend. Each one of these, by themselves, tells you very little. In fact, any long-term study of the mere number of issues rising or falling will produce little in the way of insight or predictive value. When the two are studied together, however, you can get a sense of the longer-term market sentiment.

KEY POINT

As useful as it is to divide volume between advancing and declining issues, you need to remember that this indicator is an estimation, and not a mathematically reliable one.

Consider tracking the two numbers on the same chart, perhaps dividing the chart with "zero" as a center horizontal point. Place the number of advancing issues above the center line and the number of declining issues below, using a moving average of ten weeks (for example). The visual results of this comparative study will indicate shifts in market sentiment. As the number of advancing issues tends to increase, the short-term sign is positive; if the overall tendency is dominated by declining issues, the opposite is true.

One useful variation of the advance/decline study is called the *absolute breadth index*. This is a factor representing the difference between the number of advancing issues and the number of declining issues. In this study, whether the value is positive or negative is not considered important; in other words, it does not matter whether there are more advancing or declining issues. The purpose to the absolute breadth index is to study the relative degree of difference. The theory behind this analysis states that when the absolute number is high, it is a sign that the overall trend is at a top or bottom and that the trend will soon reverse itself. So this study might help you to discover or even anticipate impending change. It should be studied in a moving average, of course, remembering that it is the larger trend and not the daily outcome that matters.

KEY POINT

The absolute breadth index is not intended to show positive or negative trends, but to signal likely tops or bottoms to current cycles or movements.

Yet another tool for studying advancing and declining issues is called the *advance/decline line*. Unlike the values in a period-by-period study, the daily net difference between advancing and declining issues is added to or subtracted from the previous day's running total. This provides you with a running "count" index starting at a base line of your own choosing. You can begin at zero and then calculate daily changes, yielding positive or negative results, or pick some arbitrary numerical level and adjust it each day.

Of what analytical value is this line method? In some respects, it provides advantages over other methods. It is simple to calculate and works as an ever-growing moving average. Because you begin at an arbitrary point (zero or some other number), the cumulative effect of the advance/decline line is indeed a moving average that requires only a simple addition or subtraction each day. This analysis also is comprehended easily, and yet it summarizes the entire market. A drawback of the advance/decline line is that the longer the period of study, the less accurate it becomes. Your starting point is arbitrary, and so that point, by itself, has no actual significance in relation to other trading days or seasons. The market's cycle, like all cycles, has starting and ending points, but the advance/decline line study begins or ends whenever it is convenient for you. With this in mind, it makes sense to periodically start over again so that your data is not based on old and outdated stock market trading levels.

Yet another variation of the advance/decline study is the *advance/decline ratio*, which, as its name implies, is a comparison between the number of advancing issues and declining issues, expressed as a ratio value in decimal or percentage form. A ten-day moving average is used commonly, with the percentage representing the result achieved by dividing advancing issues by declining issues. If the moving average of the advance/decline ratio moves higher than 1.25 (125%), the market is considered too high, or overbought. This is a bearish sign. If the average moves below 0.75 (75%), it is considered a buying opportunity, and is a bullish indicator. Everything in between is neutral.

The formula for the advance/decline ratio is:

$$\frac{\text{number of advancing issues}}{\text{number of declining issues}} = \text{ratio}$$

Volume Studies

In addition to conducting price studies, you should study volume, which is a revealing market factor that often anticipates short-term price changes. But how should you study volume? In any study, it is important to recognize the relationship between

KEY POINT

Analysis of price trends without also considering volume is a mistake. Volume is more revealing because it often anticipates coming price direction and change.

price and volume. In the previous section we demonstrated that even price analysis can be elusive: Should you study high/low trends, advance/decline trends, odd lot trading, or just price alone? Whatever specific indicators you select for inclusion in your personal analysis of the market, you also will need to include volume studies, because volume can and does predict price movement changes.

But that does not answer the important question of *how* to study volume. One way is to watch trends established in mutual fund activity. Mutual funds trade in large increments of stock. A block of 10,000 or more shares is called a large block, and the *large block ratio* is an indicator worth analyzing. To calculate, divide the trading volume of large blocks by the total volume on the exchange. The answer is expressed as a percentage. (New York Stock Exchange data is found in *The Wall Street Journal* each day.) The formula for the large block ratio is:

$$\frac{\text{large block volume}}{\text{total volume}} = \text{ratio}$$

This indicator is a good example of how volume analysis can be used to track price and even to anticipate a change in direction. The large block ratio is believed to signal points when the market is oversold or overbought, meaning that a turn is about to occur. (Oversold refers to a condition in which the market, overall, is low, and overbought means it has risen too high.)

The sense among those who follow this indicator is that institutional investors usually are wrong about the market conditions and tend to buy when they should sell and vice versa. If this belief is justified, then watching large block trading patterns is, indeed, an excellent sentiment indicator and contrarian approach. Institutional investors represent such a large percentage of the entire market that there is always the likelihood that their trading patterns actually lead the market. And because the majority usually is wrong, mutual fund activity represents a likely "wrong" opinion at any given time. Because of this, the indicator signals change and can be useful.

KEY POINT

The institutional investors, such as mutual funds, usually are wrong in their decisions, so the contrarian approach is a smart one. Use indicators relating to mutual funds by doing the opposite, and you are statistically more likely to be right.

Analyze big block volume using a moving average. A five-week average is considered reasonable, so that you can judge at what point you believe it is time to change strategies. Some observation of the cause and effect of large block trading and resultant price changes will work as a good indicator for you.

Another useful method for studying volume is the *cumulative volume index*. This is similar to the absolute breadth index in that it is a number representing the net difference between upside and downside. The difference is that this index calculates volume rather than the number of changing issues. First, subtract downside volume from upside volume. (The *downside volume* is the total volume of trading in stocks that lost value, while the *upside volume* is the total trading volume in stocks that rose in value.) If the result is a positive number, it is added to the cumulative total from the prior day and, if negative, it is subtracted. The trend, rather than any specific daily change in the net total is the key. Remember that the distinction between advancing and declining volume is inaccurate in and of itself, because stocks cannot be defined purely as being in one group or another; it is a mix of activity, the result of which ends up rising or falling. For example, a particular stock might rise only ⅟₁₆th of a point, but on very heavy volume, whereas another could fall 10, 12, or more points on relatively light volume. A comparison between these two stocks is obviously flawed. This is why you need to consider the overall market, use moving averages, and draw conclusions from trends, not from daily entries.

It might be revealing to track absolute breadth (between advancing and declining issues) on the same chart with cumulative volume, looking not so much for changes in direction but for variation in the degree of change between the number of issues and total volume. The results might produce interesting interpretations, which can be borne out only by comparing the study to resulting price movement.

What Formulas Reveal

Any study of market trends involving the use of formulas has to be viewed as part of a larger and more insightful analytical program. It is easy to forget that the purpose of overall market studies is to judge the mood of the market and to anticipate overall trends and changes in price direction. Ultimately, you will use the information to make decisions about your own portfolio, which will include a limited number of stocks.

The overall market trend cannot indicate what intermediate- or long-term changes you can expect in individual stocks. It may

KEY POINT

Formulas by themselves are of no value in managing your portfolio. They should serve as an additional source of information, not as the sole source of information.

only provide you with one form of information about potential short-term reaction to larger market forces that might not be entirely understood, and that probably do not relate directly to the investment value or growth potential of your own stocks. The formulas reveal short-term current mood and trend so that you can time your investment decisions wisely or at least with more information than you have by looking at a stock's facts and figures alone. The technical and fundamental information you have on a particular company and its stock should serve as the primary source for information and should be used for making decisions. Larger market trends only help you to pinpoint and estimate cyclical phases in the overall market.

Every investor should realize that the cycles of the market will affect a stock's value. When the market tendency is bullish, stocks tend to rise with the averages; when it is bearish, stocks tend to fall. The expression "A rising tide lifts all boats" is applicable to the market. Even though the overall trend and mood has nothing to do with a company's current fundamental status, you have to acknowledge that the market changes and moves through cycles for its own reasons and at its own pace.

The formulas dealing with price and volume in the large sense are useful in taking the temperature of the market, and that is all they are good for. It is a mistake to begin believing that, in some manner, any technical analysis of the number of issues changing, the volume trend, or overall cyclical movement can be used alone to make wise investment decisions; these analyses only yield useful bits of information that need to be placed in the more extensive puzzle of your portfolio. Because you have to consider so many factors about your stocks, the basic decisions of buy, hold, or sell (or stay out of the market) depend on numerous sources of information: financial, management, competitive, industry, chart patterns, your own bias, and intuition, to name a few. The formulas introduced earlier in this chapter serve as another source of information. Given all of the knowledge you gather directly relating to a particular company, the ultimate decision could be bolstered or contradicted by what you discover about the technical condition of the market.

The Value of Technical Indicators

The real value of technical indicators is derived from how you make use of them. One of the frequent errors made by investors is narrowing their analytical gaze too much, and then making investment decisions based on information that does not really provide them the means for informed decision making. In other words, technical information can easily be misapplied. But when applied properly, indicators are useful in a number of ways.

Comparisons between Individual Stocks and the Overall Market

One excellent method for evaluating stocks is to first determine how reactive they are to overall market forces. This is not restricted to the *beta* of a stock, which is the volatility of a stock in comparison with overall market movement. It also includes the study of the relationship between volume and price, and the tendency of the stock to react on the one hand to its own fundamentals (profits, dividends, sales, etc.) and on the other hand to outside influences, such as changing interest rates, Dow Jones Industrial Average (DJIA) swings, and market rumors.

KEY POINT

Formulas should be used to compare stocks to overall markets, as a means for judging your decisions and timing.

Comparisons between Stocks within an Industry

One important factor respected both by fundamental and technical-minded investors and analysts is the importance of the relative strength of a company within its industry. Many industries have recognized leaders, but over time that leadership position changes.

Consider the past position of IBM in comparison with the ever-changing computer industry and the emergence of other leading companies such as Hewlett-Packard and Microsoft. While the latter companies enjoyed popularity for some years, nothing is permanent in the market. In the uncertain and volatile world of tech stocks, IBM has recently emerged once again as a leader in the industry. As Microsoft has grown in industry influence, some of its policies have made the once highly favored innovator a target of government antitrust investigation, not to mention disfavor among disgruntled users *and* investors. The point is, today's leaders are not necessarily permanent; and of equal importance, the disgraced or fallen shining stars of the past may rise again. There is no magic answer; rather, you need to apply the analytical strategies and techniques that provide indication of what is likely to happen in the future.

KEY POINT

The study of industry trends is helpful because it enables you to recognize when today's leading companies are beginning to slip and give way to others.

Comparisons between Industries

Another valuable analytical tool is the study of different industries. Just as companies within one industry gain and lose leadership positions, particular industries rise and fall in the approval

KEY POINT

Industries, like individual stocks, rise and fall in popularity with the investing public. Recognizing the subtle signs of change helps you become an informed investor.

game with investors. Today's industry leaders might lead the market into ever-higher growth levels, or down into record depths, all depending on where that influence lies. And like individual companies and their competitors, different industries rise and fall over time.

Comparisons from One Period to Another for the Purpose of Spotting Turns in Market Cycles

You know that all market changes occur in cycles that are predictable, although the timing and extent of those cycles cannot be known in advance. It is essential, therefore, that you not only follow the price and volume trends of individual stocks, but also that you become aware of larger market cycles. A study of volume- and price-specific formulas using a form of trend analysis can help you to anticipate likely cyclical changes in the market, which is especially valuable to the extent that your portfolio is affected for good or bad by those changes. Through study, you gain a sense of the rhythm in the market, and that is where your investment insights come from.

KEY POINT

The study of market-wide trends is essential for recognizing the less obvious and subtle shifts in cyclical timing of the overall market.

Early Signals of Potential Changes in the Near Future

The successful investor does not follow, but rather leads. You require early signals to know before "the herd" does what might happen tomorrow or the next day. But even that is not enough. You also need the determination and confidence to act decisively and quickly, before others realize the change and act, by which time it is too late. Successful investors use early signals and act on them, even though the reality is that acting against the majority is somewhat intimidating. The majority is usually wrong, but acting with them provides great comfort and the illusion of safety. It is an illusion because in reality there is no safety in being wrong most of the time.

KEY POINT

The illusion of safety in following the majority is just that, an illusion. Successful investing requires that you break away and think for yourself—as a means of profiting more than the average investor.

Pitfalls in Using Formulas

The major pitfall in using formulas is that you might lose sight of your real purpose. Formulas study overall markets but tell you nothing about your own portfolio. They look at larger averages and trends, but the pieces of information within the larger market are unreliable and inaccurate for your purposes.

For example, imagine trying to analyze the volume for a specific stock using upside and downside days only. The results might be interesting to track, but they would provide you with no real population or sample for statistical reliability. It would be comparable to taking a poll by asking questions of only one person. You need a larger sample to judge what is going on.

The formulas studying volume and price tell you what the mood is within the market in general. They reflect sentiment at a given moment, providing a "confidence index" that shows relative degrees of optimism or pessimism as a snapshot in time. This result is not necessarily indicative of the direction of a larger trend; it only represents the latest entry in a trend—and you cannot even be certain that the trend is helpful to you for investing in your portfolio.

KEY POINT

Every market-wide indicator is an entry in a larger trend, whose reliability depends largely on how it is used.

What do you do about market mood? Does a pessimistic mood make your well-chosen investments less attractive? Or does an optimistic mood make a poor-performing stock more promising? Of course not. The formula only tells you what the opinion is within the market, and it is elusive even with the formula. You cannot be sure that the current price or volume trend really does reflect opinion, because it includes the effects of the economy, politics, domestic and international tensions, and much more. And even the obsession with the unreliable and inaccurate DJIA distorts the opinion within the market. The varying levels of stock splits make some companies more influential than others, for example, so fundamentals of those companies distort the DJIA, which most people consider to be "the market" even with its unreliability. Even many well-informed investors really have not stopped to think about how unreliable the Dow is for the purposes of judging the market.

The real popularity of the DJIA is derived from its ease of use. Investors do not have to calculate anything because it is given to them ready to go. Reporters in the financial press tell people what the changes mean, even when they do not know themselves— *because the changes do not mean anything.* An example of how the DJIA distorts the real mood of the market is seen whenever it approaches record territory, especially if that record is divisible by 1,000, for example, the 8,000, 9,000, or 10,000 level. At such times, there is a tendency for the DJIA to have exceptionally high point days, because there is a sentiment among investors (notably among institutional investors) to reach and pass those bellwether points.

KEY POINT

The DJIA is thought by most to represent the market. Unfortunately, this idea is misleading and inaccurate—and wrong.

Why is this? Think about the motivation of a mutual fund for a moment. The fund's management knows that when the market reaches a major threshold (like the 10,000-point level), many first-time investors flock to the market enthusiastically, wanting to get their money in while the market is hot. And of course, there are always a record number of new investors at market peaks. So such peaks are great for mutual fund management whose compensation is based on dollars invested in their funds. One point is worth remembering, though: Because the DJIA is an index with an arbitrary starting point, the bellwether phases have absolutely no meaning. Even forgetting for the moment the important observation that the DJIA is terribly flawed and inaccurate, the point value of the market has no value or meaning. It is arbitrary.

There is an almost shameful element to the so-called professional investment adviser who is interviewed on financial television or radio shows or in the financial press, and is asked the inevitable question, "Where do you think the Dow is headed?" Another variation is, "Do you think the Dow will go over (fill in the blank) this

KEY POINT

One of the more troubling failings of the financial press is that it keeps alive the idea that Dow watching is a meaningful and important activity. The same problem is found with most so-called experts.

year?" An honest response would be to explain that the market, as measured by the Dow, has no meaning—the real measure of the market's health is seen in the fundamentals and market prices of individual stocks—and that judging the health of the market with an arbitrary and inaccurate index is flawed thinking.

By the same argument, using formulas that establish baselines and then test and compare the number of issues, rising and falling volume, or price against those baselines should be seen as one of many forms of information, *not* as the last word.

Maximizing the Technical Approach

With the point of view that index watching is a flawed practice, how can you actually make the best use of technical information? In truth, there is nothing wrong with the technical indicators themselves; the point here is only that they should be used intelligently, and that all too often they come to represent the sum total of a program. The worst offenders are the experts themselves, whose motivation is to increase their subscription base or readership. There are plenty of information sources, including highly reliable ones—on the Internet and in person— and for very little cost. The real challenge to maximizing technical information is determining how it can best be used. The truly wise investor does not merely have a lot of information or knowledge available. She also knows its purpose and its limits.

To ensure that you maximize your technical approach to investing, follow these nine basic guidelines:

1. *Never allow yourself to limit your analysis to only one indicator.* The most common error made by investors is failing to expand their analytical horizons beyond one easily understood, readily available, and simple indicator like the DJIA. Use as many indicators as you need, while also recognizing that you need to limit the scope of your analysis to remain effective.

KEY POINT

Do not take the easy route the Dow watchers use. Find indicators that really provide you with information that increases your profits.

2. *Always confirm a conclusion independently.* No isolated, solitary bit of information is all-revealing. Everything you learn from analysis needs to be confirmed or counterindicated independently. Just as the latest entry in a trend is only that and not the whole story, no single bit of information can tell you all that you need to know about timing your decisions.

KEY POINT

Never fall into the mistaken belief that any one form of information is the whole story. Confirm and verify everything before acting.

3. *Learn from observation about how technical indicators today compare to price changes tomorrow.* Perhaps the most valuable thing you learn from a study of technical indicators is how accurately you judge and time your decisions. The experience of interpretation is not in how it leads you to higher levels of accuracy, but in what it teaches you about the inaccuracy of any form of forecasting. The experienced analyst understands all too well how unreliable forecasting is no matter how much good information you have.

KEY POINT

It is not enough to gather information efficiently. It is equally important to analyze what you concluded yesterday, and to advance your analytical skills by learning from your mistakes.

4. *Recognize that price and volume studies about overall markets tell you nothing about your portfolio.* Profoundly, and to some people surprisingly, overall trends in the market reveal nothing about how you should invest and when (or if) you should buy or sell shares of stock. This observation, while true, will anger some analysts who would prefer to believe that there is some magic answer to everything, and that the answer will be found in more detailed analysis and study of overall markets. That simply is not true.

KEY POINT

When it comes to your portfolio, overall market trends are of no use. The argument that investment decisions should be made based on market-wide analysis is simply wrong.

5. *Stop watching the DJIA as a representation of the market and recognize it as only one reflection of market sentiment, and not as an accurate technical indicator.* The inaccuracy of the DJIA is easily proved, but even so, investors and market professionals are obsessed with the number itself. When it passes through a level divisible by 1,000, there is applause and celebration on the floor of the New York

KEY POINT

The numbers game practiced on Wall Street is foolish and meaningless. The DJIA is of no use in the intelligent management of your portfolio.

Stock Exchange, whose members should know better, and probably do.

6. *Always defer to analysis of the company, rather than using broader indicators that do not help you with the four basic decisions: buy, hold, sell, or stay out.* Even the most ardent technician needs to return to the fundamentals for reliable stock-specific information. The purpose of technical analysis is to provide useful information by indicating and confirming overall directions, not to replace the undeniable value of fundamental analysis.

KEY POINT

When all is said and done, individual investment decisions require a study of the fundamentals. Technical analysis is valuable for confirmation, but not as a sole or isolated source.

7. *Do your own research and don't depend on others; think for yourself.* There is a lot of information out there, some valuable and some mere junk. You certainly can employ good sources of information, such as thorough research and analysis found through subscription services or on the Internet, to enhance your knowledge bank. However, when you use research prepared by someone else, do not just accept their conclusions. Think for yourself and look at the

KEY POINT

You should perform your own research; otherwise, you might as well just ask someone else what you should do. Those who invest by having others tell them what to do have no right to expect to do better than the average investor. And "average" is not profitable.

entire lass of research you develop, rather than just taking at face value what someone else decides.

8. *Be suspicious of extremely good news that you were not expecting.* In all forms of research, the astute analyst has a fairly good idea about what to expect. The analyst looks for signals of change that require action, and those signals often come about in small increments. The sudden, dramatic, flashing-red-light kind of indicator is very rare. So if and when you discover big change, notably when it is good news for you, examine your material once more. Chances are good that there is a mistake, a false or misleading indicator, or some other error that should be corrected, especially when the news is not confirmed elsewhere.

KEY POINT

Obvious information is already known to the market as a whole by the time it has become obvious, meaning there is no advantage to be had by acting. If you know for certain that the indicator is true, it's too late.

9. *Trust your intuition. Look beyond the numbers.* Even with a vast array of information, you can still make mistakes; in fact, you can depend upon it. The information itself,

remember, is only for the purpose of indicating what is likely or probable. Ultimately, you can never know precisely what will happen ahead of time. Thus, even the best information is flawed because it represents estimation about the future, not precise pointers. With this in mind, do not ignore your own intuition. Act on your sense of what will work and, of equal importance, avoid situations in which your intuition tells you there is too much risk. Intuition is a valid tool.

KEY POINT

Never ignore a gut feeling. Your intuition is the sum of your knowledge and experience and can be used to warn yourself about high-risk situations or to recognize opportunities.

CHAPTER 8

Sentiment Indicators

The ruling force in the market is neither logical nor sound. The market is not fueled by the fundamentals, the nuts and bolts of sales and profits, or the financial prospects of a corporation or the quality of its management. The market is run by opinion—an elusive perception of future potential that invariably is wrong, even to the point of being *entirely* wrong.

This opinion at large is measured in several ways through *sentiment indicators*, which are meant to gauge the mood of the market. Investors are at times fearful about rising interest rates, political unrest, or economic bad news. At other times, they might be euphoric about the rosy future, believing that a booming economy will never end and every stock will continue rising forever. Both of these opinions, of course, are extreme, and there

KEY POINT

Sentiment, or mood, rules the market and determines how investors feel—in spite of the real economic news or financial situation.

never is a universal mood. However, with consistency a particular sentiment rules at any given time and the market can be measured by that sentiment.

The two extremes of sentiment are fear and greed. When investors are fearful, stock prices are down and the fear is that they might continue to fall. The greater the level of fear and pessimism, the greater the likelihood that the majority opinion is wrong, because it almost always is wrong. When markets are at all-time high levels, the greed factor takes over. People who have never been in the market want to get in on the profit, and those already in will do anything to increase their holdings. The more money that is earned, the greater the mood of greed. In fact, one popular contrary indicator tied to sentiment is a measure of the number of first-time investors. The belief is that first-time investors enter the market in big numbers from a sense of naïve greed; and when the number of first-time investors increases, it signals a market top and impending bearish conditions. There is some historical support for this belief.

KEY POINT

The majority is usually wrong, so a popular investing method is to gauge sentiment and then go with the opposite. This is more easily said than done.

It is not easy to make decisions contrary to the majority, although it is the logical choice once you realize that the majority usually is wrong. When fear dominates the market, however, it makes sense to worry and to experience that fear yourself, even if you know that conditions mandate taking action. In such conditions, when prices are severely depressed and the news is all bad, the logical choice is to buy; but the fear factor might prevent you from acting. And when the mood of the market is greedy, it is difficult to ignore the apparent potential for fast profits and make the logical decision—to sell and wait on the sidelines.

Short Interest Ratio

Even when you understand the contrarian approach—that you should often make decisions in opposition to the majority—it is not easy to know exactly how to measure sentiment. There are a number of popular indicators that you can use. First among these is the *short interest ratio*. Short interest is the number of shares sold short, a number that is published in the financial press and available on the Internet.* Investors who sell short execute transactions in a method opposite the commonly understood sequence of buy, hold, and sell. A short seller first sells stock and then, after waiting for some period of time, buys the same number of shares. In that sequence, the last step—buying the stock—closes the transaction. Short selling is done when investors believe the market price is high and will fall in the future. Thus, stock can be sold for today's market price and purchased later at a lower price, with the difference representing a profit on the transaction.

Short interest, or the total number of shares sold short, is a useful sentiment indicator. When the number of short interest shares is high, it is a bearish signal—and obviously, the more shares sold, the more bearish. It indicates a higher degree of belief that prices will fall in the near future. The opposite also is true. When short interest falls, it indicates a bullish mood, a reflection of the belief among investors that prices are going to rise rather than fall.

To calculate short interest ratio, divide the number of shares sold short by total volume during the same period.

$$\frac{\text{number of shares sold short}}{\text{total volume traded}} \ = \ \text{ratio}$$

An interesting fine-tuning of this analysis is the *members' short index*. Stock exchange member trading is interesting to

---

*For short interest and other useful statistics on current trading (as well as names and addresses of the major stock exchanges), check www.cftech.com/BrainBank/FINANCE/NewYorkStockExch.html.

watch because, unlike the market as a whole, members of the stock exchanges tend to be right more than wrong. So when the short interest among members is contradicted by the overall short interest, it provides you with some insight and could be used as a contrarian indicator. For example, if the overall short interest is higher than average but the members' short index is lower than average, it may be wiser to follow the lead of members rather than the market as a whole. The New York Stock Exchange (NYSE) publishes information on member transactions every week.

Margin Debt

Another interesting statistic to follow is the level of *margin debt*. While this reflects changing trends in the flow of funds within the market, it also reveals a lot about the sentiment among margin investors.

Margin debt is the amount of money borrowed by investors and brokers, with securities left on account as collateral. The borrowed money is then invested in more securities. As a general rule, margin debt levels tend to rise along with rising prices, and to fall as prices also fall. Margin debt accurately reflects the mood of the market that also is seen in bullish and bearish tendencies. In that respect, it is an indicator of market levels of fear and greed.

KEY POINT

Fear and greed rule the market, so margin debt is a good test not only of bulls and bears, but also of greed and fear—the pigs and chickens of the market.

Margin debt is published by exchanges as well as by the major brokerage houses. In historical perspective, margin debt levels have worked as good indicators in tracking market sentiment, and could be used to anticipate upcoming changes in market direction. However, margin debt is not a free-rein indicator. Margin requirements are set by federal law and changing interest rates might have more to do with growing or declining levels of margin debt than actual bull or bear sentiment. However, because interest rates also affect market sentiment, it could be argued that margin debt is a reliable indicator even when changes in interest rates encourage higher levels or lower levels.

Other Sentiment Indicators and What They Reveal

The most interesting sentiment indicator might be the majority opinion of the market. This opinion is wrong most of the time. So you can judge the market mood correctly simply by reading the financial press, which reports the majority opinion and, because of that, is usually wrong as well. By tracking the majority opinion and then adopting a contrary strategy, you will be right more often than wrong.

KEY POINT

Because the majority is wrong more often than not, it is logical to disagree with the majority. Ironically, this is a difficult stand for many because the majority is a compelling force, even when it is wrong.

It is ironic that the majority opinion serves as such a reliable indicator, but that also explains why the contrarian approach is so popular. Because the majority is most often wrong, it is logical to contradict that majority opinion. Because it is easy to tell what the majority thinks, such an opinion is easily discovered without having to compute moving average or analyze and interpret a trend. This opinion cannot be placed on a chart, but if you are active in the market, you already know the general mood among other investors. The difficult part is not determining the opinion of the market as a whole, it is having the confidence to take an approach that places you in the minority.

Most people want to be accepted by others, and will take comfort in going along with the majority. This might explain why the majority is wrong so often. For example, we have previously cited studies showing that mutual funds beat the Standard & Poor's 500 (S&P 500) only about one-tenth of the time. This dismal record is not surprising, given the size and influence of mutual funds.

Acting as a contrarian—on its surface—means going against the majority. However, this does not mean that you should blindly contradict every majority opinion that comes along, but only that you should recognize that as a sentiment indicator the majority tends to move in the wrong direction more often than not. As a contrarian, follow these four guidelines:

1. *Begin with the premise of mistrusting the majority.* Most people start with the premise that the majority is right. This is the first mistake investors make. As uncomfortable as it feels to take a minority view, you need to remember that this is the first step in developing an independent and analytical point of view. It is a requirement of success in the market that you think for yourself rather than follow the usually flawed lead of the market in general.

KEY POINT

The premise that the majority is right is flawed, but, ironically, it is a comfortable belief, and so it has many subscribers.

2. *Confirm all information independently before you act.* No one should trust blindly, because that is how you lose in the market. Nothing is so simple that it can just be adhered to without intelligent thought and analysis. The fact that the majority is wrong more than it is right does not mean that you should automatically do the opposite of the majority in each and every case. Your observation of majority actions is but one of many indicators that provides you with good information. The degree of faith you place in the observation should vary according to the circumstances.

KEY POINT

There is a tendency to seek the kind of information we want, and then to act on it. Rather, we should seek reliable information, and then go to whatever lengths required to confirm it before we act.

3. *Recognize that experts do not really know what is going to happen.* The market is full of experts. It is in vogue for many experts to refer to themselves as contrarians, even when they are not. The experts, like everyone else, tend to imitate one another and to follow rather than lead. True leaders are rare—in the market as everywhere else. The insight that experts really do not know what is going to happen any more than anyone else, while obvious, can be

KEY POINT

One of the more troubling insights is that experts do not know what they are doing. It means that you are on your own.

helpful in developing your independent market mind. If they did know, would they not be rich? Why do they have to sell their opinions?

4. *Keep your mind open to all market theories and possibilities.* The contrarian approach is a valuable one because it is a logical response to the proven reality that the majority is most often wrong. Because that is the case, it makes sense to act as a contrarian. However, "even a paranoid has some real enemies"* and, by the same logic, even the majority can be right sometimes. No theory should be applied blindly. The key to successful analysis is to develop an intelligent approach, which means a thinking approach, one that allows for a range of possible meanings of information and does not attempt to simplify everything down to an easily followed formula.

KEY POINT

To serve as your own best analyst, you need to be open to any and all possibilities. When you are, your approach is scientific and resistant to bias.

Measuring the Mood of the Market

The purely mathematical spirit wants to reduce everything to a formula. Such an analytical mind takes great comfort in the certainty of a trend line, the dependability of a moving average, and the simple absolute nature of an equation. But interestingly enough, the market is not so easily reduced and studied. Sentiment indicators are not absolutes; they are highly intangible and cannot be reduced to formulas.

---

*Henry Kissinger, in *Newsweek*, June 13, 1983.

Some attempts have been made to reduce sentiment indicators to formula form. Many of the reliable sentiment indicators, such as short interest ratio, can in fact be studied in this way. But to really measure the mood of the market, you need to talk to people, read the financial press, and study. Beyond watching stock prices and volume trends, you need to understand how the intangible moods and opinions of the market—right or wrong—change over time. You cannot reduce to a reliable formula the many factors at work—rumors and gossip, financial reports, economic factors such as interest rate changes, political news, regulatory change, mergers, and the dozens of other *known* causes—not to mention the unknown influences that also are at work in the market. And at times, a particular mood or opinion just exists without any analytical reason that can be identified.

In this respect, the sentiment of the market operates on a cycle of its own, and it might be the most mysterious of all market-related cycles because there are no known numerical or financial causes that can be studied to better understand it. The sentiment cycle is reflected in price swings, especially those of primary movements, as well as in volume and other measurements. But the timing of market mood and opinion cannot be judged or anticipated mathematically. So for the exceptionally high number of analytical personalities who invest in the stock market, sentiment, and all that it implies, is the most troubling factor of all. It cannot be quantified, weighted, or even studied with any reliable methods.

KEY POINT

Some things, such as the mood of the market, cannot be measured mathematically. They have to be observed and studied without the certainty of a formula.

It is, nonetheless, very real. It can be seen, heard, and felt in the financial press, among brokers and investors, and in business offices around America. People's moods do affect the market and everyone in it. But we all have to accept the problems connected with sentiment. It is not a tangible factor and yet it is very real.

Using Averages to Assess Mood

Some averaging techniques can be useful in assessing the mood of the market. We have mentioned the short interest ratio as an example of how this is done. But even a reliable and historically accurate ratio such as this does not really assess mood as much as it reports it. Thus, it is more of a backward-looking analysis. Technicians prefer indicators that anticipate and predict, because accurate information about what has not yet occurred is far more interesting and useful than a mere study of what was caused by yesterday's moods.

You might apply the moving average technique to some aspects of sentiment. To the extent that sentiment is caused or changed by more tangible factors, such as interest rates and other economic statistics, it might be possible to track and even anticipate sentiment. The key to this is the moving average and the observation of economic cycles. Remembering that timing of economic change is uncertain, whereas the cycles and their changes are inevitable, it still is possible to track the cycles of the economy and to anticipate some forms of change.

KEY POINT

The tracking of sentiment is elusive and of questionable value—but still fascinating, because sentiment *is* the market in so many respects.

For example, you might observe a tendency for interest rates to rise and fall with a degree of predictability. A study of stock market trends (or sentiment) reveals that rising or falling interest rates often precede major shifts in price movement. Does this reflect sentiment? Of course it does, if only because everything that affects the market and the prices of stocks also affects sentiment. The market sentiment is like a sponge that absorbs everything and, all too often, overinterprets it. The market as a whole becomes euphoric over even the smallest amount of good news, and falls into a dark pit of gloom over similarly minor bad news—only to forget about it and bounce back the next moment. Recognizing the overreactive, perhaps even irrational, nature of the market, a study of sentiment using a moving average might be possible. By tracking factors such as interest rates and then studying the lagging effect on stock price levels and movement trends, you might be able to arrive at a charted version of what you could call sentiment. By this definition, sentiment would represent the dynamic relationship between the outside economic influence and the resulting change in price direction, or the variation in degree of movement caused by that influence.

Confidence and Misery Indexes

Another way to assess mood is with the *confidence index*. A widely followed and popular indicator, it was developed by the financial weekly publication *Barron's* in 1932. The ratio is the result of dividing the average yield of high-grade bonds by the average yield of intermediate-grade bonds.

The premise underlying the confidence index is that investors take higher risks when they have a higher degree of confidence or optimism, and that as their fears increase they invest more conservatively. It might seem odd to judge stock market sentiment by an indicator that is based entirely on bonds; however, a direct tie between the two markets has been observed. When investors are optimistic, they display a greater tendency to invest in the stock market than they do when their confidence level is low; thus, confidence as a market factor has the effect

KEY POINT

In spite of the problems associated with tracking confidence among investors, such efforts have been underway for some time—with an unsurprising lack of historical value.

of driving up stock prices. In that respect, it is fair to observe that when investors feel good about the economy and its prospects for the future, their confidence leads them to invest, and the demand reflected in the greater investment level drives up stock prices.

This point of view is somewhat contrary to the belief that confidence grows from the successful stock investing reflected in bull markets. That point of view holds that rising stock prices bolster confidence. Both points of view have elements of truth, and there can be little doubt that while a healthy economy and rising stock prices accompany one another, one does not cause the other.

Although the confidence index has been around for many decades, current opinion about it is not high. It does not hold a reliable record for establishing trends or confirming current market mood. It might be that the relationship between bond yields and stock market activity is somewhat distant, and that the multitude of factors creating and driving stock market trends is too complex to be anticipated by such a remote indicator.

KEY POINT

The confidence index is not a reliable indicator, and yet it continues to be published and cited—evidence of how the market operates in spite of what little science there is to prove many ideas.

Another index of some interest is the *misery index*. This is a calculation using three separate economic statistics: prime rate, inflation rate, and unemployment rate. As might be expected, the misery index tends to work as a mirror opposite of price trends in the market—when the market is high, the misery index is low, and vice versa. This is not a magic formula, but a reflection of the economy's influence on the market. The misery index tracks the economy's effect on prices, but serves no more value for prediction than price charts themselves.

In addition to lacking forecasting properties, the misery index is flawed by the nature of its components. The prime rate, which is the rate banks charge to their most favored customers, does not always reflect the true health of the money supply or of the competition for borrowed money. The federal funds rate might be a more accurate measurement of economic health concerning interest rates, even though prime rate is a favored means for measuring interest trends. The inflation rate also is deserving of criticism. The Consumer Price Index (CPI) is the normal method used to define inflation, and is compiled with what the Department of Labor considers a typical range of consumer purchases. The CPI has many inaccuracies, which could mean inflation is understated or overstated, depending on which studies are cited. The definition of inflation is far more elusive than would be suggested by the summary report reducing inflation to a simple percentage. The third element, the unemployment rate, also is flawed because it never reflects the true condition of unemployment. It is a compilation only of the individuals who apply for benefits. It does not include those out of work who have not applied or those who have been unemployed for so long that they are no longer considered in the statistic.

KEY POINT

The misery index depends on directly related economic indicators, and therefore might provide reliable ideas about general mood.

None of this is meant to suggest that the misery index is inefficient in presenting the mood of the economy. In spite of the consistency of the flaws in the statistics studied, the misery index probably serves as well as any other measurement to demonstrate the mood of the economy, and to demonstrate how varying degrees of negative influence are reflected in market price trends. The point worth making, though, is that the misery index really does not tell you anything with forecasting value, or anything that can be used to effectively make decisions about managing your stock portfolio.

KEY POINT

While the misery index is helpful in identifying mood, remember that it combines three unrelated economic statistics. It is possible that the three counteract each other at times, reducing the effectiveness of the index.

Economic Indicators and Market Mood

The negative indicators mentioned above—prime rate, inflation, and unemployment—are not the only economic indicators that can reflect the mood of the market. The following also serve as excellent sentiment indicators.

Gross National Product (GNP)

Gross National Product, or GNP, is a broad measurement of spending in the United States that is widely accepted as the most dependable measure of the economy. It measures the total "productivity" or economic output by considering two different elements: demand and income. It measures markets for goods and services to determine demand, and it measures the cost of producing goods and services to determine income. These methods also are called demand and supply methods. Under the demand method, a breakdown involves personal expenditures, investments, net exports, and government purchases—in other words, the sources of demand for goods and services. Under the income, or supply method, income is broken down in several broad categories: earnings of employees, rental income, corporate profits, interest, and sales and property taxes, for example. A subset of the GNP is the Gross Domestic Product, or GDP, a report limited to activity of the GNP occurring only within the United States and excluding all foreign trade and activity.

KEY POINT

The GNP is a measurement of real supply and demand, and is a popularly cited reference for the measurement of sentiment. It reflects willingness to spend (demand) and production levels (supply) in the U.S. economy.

Producer Price Index (PPI)

The Producer Price Index, or PPI, is similar to the CPI, but calculated at the wholesale level. It might serve as a more accurate measurement of inflation than the CPI, because the CPI reflects marked-up values, which is inconsistent between products and between regions. However, PPI is not used as the public referral point for measuring inflation. The Department of Labor compiles statistics on the PPI.

KEY POINT

The PPI is more reliable for measuring inflation than the CPI because it is based on wholesale prices.

Personal Income and Expenditures

The Personal Income and Expeditures report summarizes American workers' income and expenditures each month. About two-thirds of the country's GDP is represented by personal consumption spending. This includes spending for durable goods (goods that last a long time, such as furniture and automobiles) and nondurable goods (less expensive and more easily replaced merchandise). The differences in trends between these two kinds of spending can be interpreted to have different meanings in terms of economic health, not to mention ramifications for different segments of the market.

KEY POINT

The measurement of consumer spending shows sentiment because when people feel optimistic, they want to buy; when they are afraid, they do not.

Balance of Trade

The balance of trade is in the news a lot. The measurement reflects the difference between the value of U.S. imports and exports, with the general belief that exports are better for the economy. Thus, when the import dollar amount exceeds the export dollar amount, it is considered a negative. The excess of imports over exports is called the *trade deficit,* and this deficit's effect on the value of the dollar as compared with other currencies is a constant source of concern among economists. One problem with this measurement has to do with relative sizes of consumer populations. For example, if you compare the population of the United States with that of Japan, it is obvious that the United States has a much larger population, and thus more consumers. And when compared with China, it also is obvious that the U.S. market is dwarfed by the Chinese market. It might be more accurate to compute the

KEY POINT

Balance of trade often is cited as a reliable indicator, but it is not realistic because of vastly different population levels the United States and other countries. It is not realistic to equate demand as though all countries have the same population size.

trade deficit on a per capita basis given the reality of the vast differences in population size by country.

Index of Leading Economic Indicators

A valuable compilation of indicators about the economy, and a method for judging it, is found in the Index of Leading Economic Indicators. This indicator can be used to support other technical indicators and to confirm (or contradict) what you discover about the mood of the market. While that mood might appear to be reflected in price and volume trends, evidence of optimism or pessimism about the economy can add to your bank of information.

KEY POINT

Combining different indicators has both good and bad points. It tends to help in the overall analysis of economic status, but it also tends to mask some significant changes because some indicators might contradict one another.

The Index of Leading Economic Indicators is published by the Conference Board (an economic research company with international membership), and it consists of the following 11 primary indicators, designed to collectively indicate the direction of the economy in the future:

1. *Average initial weekly claims for state unemployment insurance.* The demand for work is first reflected in unemployment insurance claims. As workers are laid off and apply for unemployment insurance benefits (or, more to the point, as the number of new applications increases or decreases), conclusions can be drawn about the direction of the current trend as well as the rapidity of the change.

2. *Average work week of production workers in manufacturing.* This indicator is thought to provide insight into the mood among production executives regarding the state of the economy. Currently employed workers' hours might be adjusted in the initial phases of a recession or recovery before employees are laid off or new workers are hired. Trends in the average work week are believed to foreshadow changes in the production economy.

3. *Building permits for new private housing units.* As construction of new homes grows, the implication is that more people are buying—a sign of strong optimism about the future. And as the number of new housing building permits declines, it indicates a weakening economy, higher unemployment, or higher interest rates, or all of the above.

4. *Change in manufacturers' unfilled orders in durable goods industries.* When companies are building inventories, they demonstrate an expectation of higher future sales. As inventory levels are reduced, it demonstrates that management expects lower sales in the near future.

5. *Change in sensitive materials prices.* Materials with long production lead time are affected by sudden changes in demand. Material prices increase with demand, so the cost of production is driven upward.

6. *Contracts and orders for plants and equipment (adjusted for inflation).* As the number of contract orders grows, the health of the economy improves, also leading to a strong need for workers in the future. As the order level falls, the reverse is

indicated in the near future: a slower economy and higher unemployment.

7. *Index of consumer expectations.* The measurement of expectations reflects sentiment among the public. This index is compiled by the Conference Board along with the University of Michigan's Survey Research Center, which develops an index of consumer confidence. The purpose of this index is to anticipate changes in the economy before they are reflected in other indicators.

8. *Manufacturers' new orders for consumer goods and materials (adjusted for inflation).* As orders for raw materials increase, it indicates growth in the economy, which also will be reflected in high levels of employment. As new order levels decrease, it also can be anticipated that unemployment and slower production levels will follow.

9. *Money supply, or M2 (adjusted for inflation).* The money supply (M2) includes savings and checking account balances plus money market investments—the total liquidity in the market. As M2 grows, so does corporate buying power and consumer tendency to buy durable goods. As M2 contracts, corporate and personal buying power decline as well.

10. *Stock prices of 500 common stocks.* Current stock price trends show investors' overall mood about the economy and are therefore a good indicator of sentiment. The stock trend also affects corporate capitalization for continued growth. When prices are up, it is relatively easy for corporations to raise funds to expand because they can sell shares for more money; when prices are down, corporations can benefit from using debt (bonds) rather than equity (stocks) to fund growth.

11. *Vendor performance.* This is a test of how quickly vendors deliver goods to manufacturers. When delivery time slows down, it indicates increased demand for materials and a strengthening economy; when vendor delivery time is faster, it indicates a slowing in the overall economy.

CHAPTER **9**

Technical Indicators
and Risk

There is great emphasis in the market, especially among commissioned salespeople and in the financial press, on the *opportunities* in the market. A lot less is mentioned about risk. And yet the two are related and cannot be separated.

Risk is a broad term covering a large area. Most of us are familiar with the best-known type, *market risk,* which, in its most basic form, is the risk that the market value of stock you buy will go down instead of up. Market risk includes much more, of course, and you also are exposed to many other forms of risk whenever you have capital to invest. Market risk includes price-related risks of missed opportunities, diversification, liquidity, and inflation. These risks are discussed further below.

When it comes to technical analysis, a lot of emphasis is placed on the specific indicators and what they are supposed to show

KEY POINT

Risk is the most important consideration in the comparison of investments, but is the one element most often overlooked.

199

you, but most indicators do not address the question of risk. The forecasting value of indicators is emphasized even though we all know that it is in trend analysis that we discover valuable predictive techniques. The risk factor, ironically, is one of the more important considerations in the selection and timing of investments, because it determines beyond anything else whether your analysis is accurate.

For example, in the evaluation of two or more different companies, what criteria do you employ to compare the stock of one to that of another? Most people are aware of the fundamental and technical indicators available to them, but what good are the best analytical tools if they are not comparable in risk? It is the quantification of risk itself that ultimately should determine the relevance of any comparisons. If your analysis involves companies with vastly dissimilar risk levels, then the potential reward levels are dissimilar as well.

To create a valid comparison base, it is essential that you also ensure the compatibility of the stocks you analyze. If the issues are not comparable, then your evaluation has to be modified with the risk levels in mind. This is the same advice a real estate agent would give to someone looking for a home. It does not make sense to compare a large apartment complex to a small, cozy cottage, or to compare a mansion on the hill with a fixer-upper in a run-down part of town. "Which of these should I buy?" would not be the right question. Rather, the homebuyer should begin by asking, "What kind of property am I looking for?"

The same is true in the stock market, although this obvious point is overlooked all too often. If you want long-term growth

KEY POINT

Stocks, like all investments, should be classified according to potential gain *and* by risk level, which is really the same thing.

stocks, you accept one risk level; if you want fast profits at the risk of sudden losses, then you are entering into an entirely different risk level and you assume a much different risk profile.

The Overlooked Aspect of Investing— Risk Management

The process of evaluating potential is simply called *analysis* by most people. Hunting for opportunities in the market is the nuts and bolts of Wall Street. It is the daily obsession of every analyst in the business as well as most investors. Of equal importance—but perhaps far less interesting—is the process of determining risk levels. This process, risk management, does not refer to the purchase of insurance. (In the insurance business, *risk management* is a marketing term used in place of the less attractive *buying insurance*.) Instead, risk is inseparable from reward potential. It is the flip side of the same coin.

You need to begin by defining the degree of risk characteristic of a specific stock in comparison with risk levels of other stocks you want to follow. Some technical indicators can be used to effectively demonstrate comparable levels of risk. Some examples follow.

Charts

Even the most basic study of charts reveals a lot about stocks and market risk. Compare charts for several stocks you are following with the same scale and period, and you will see immediately the comparison of volatility among those issues. Some stocks show a broad range of price change over a relatively small period of time, meaning they are more volatile in terms of price range; others are relatively stable during the same period.

The more volatile stocks are more interesting to track, of course, because of the degree of change, and the less volatile stocks are not very interesting at all. Differences in volatility reflect different levels of risk.

KEY POINT

A comparison between stocks with different volatility levels is not a comparison at all. There is no basis for comparison because risk as well as potential reward are dissimilar.

Volume Tests

Another way that risk levels can be reviewed visually is through charting or moving average studies of volume, especially when combined with price charting. You will observe at once that some stocks show specific patterns of the relationship between volume and price, while others seem to be entirely haphazard. The more predictable pattern provides you with a means for forecasting and the likelihood of greater predictive value in the future. If the relationship between volume and price is affected by heavy investment levels by mutual funds and other institutional investors, that is further information indicating levels of risk. You can track institutional interest in a stock as one form of technical indicator—either because you trust the judgment of fund management or, in a contrary manner, you recognize that fund management usually is wrong.

KEY POINT

The analysis of risk by using volume tests reveals some interesting trends, such as the direct relationship between volume and price among some stocks—and the complete absence of any relationship among others.

Price-Earnings Ratio

The price-earnings ratio (PE) is one of the most interesting indicators because of what it reveals and because of how it is perceived. In previous chapters, we documented the interesting study of PEs over time. Lower-PE stocks tend to outperform the market average, while higher-PE stocks tend to perform beneath the market average—but the perception among investors is much different. Whatever you make of this outcome, a comparison of PE among different stocks is a good indication of relative risk, at least as it is perceived in the market. Make sure that a comparison using PE is fairly accurate: the time since the last financial report must be approximately identical for the stocks in order for the comparison to have any meaning. If the financial report of one stock is one week old and that of the other is nearly three months old, there is absolutely no basis for comparing PEs between the two stocks. In fact, there is no basis for including any stocks with older financial reports because all of their PEs will be out of date.

KEY POINT

It is easy to overlook the inaccuracy problem of the price-earnings ratio (PE) because it is a convenient and easily understood test. But if financial information is old, the PE has no value.

Industry-Specific Comparisons

Another indicator containing both technical and fundamental elements is a comparison of values within one industry. Each industry has a leader, that company whose stock holds market value and whose sales and profits are the most favorable among the pack. But remember when studying risks that the leader is a constant target.

Also remember that things change, and today's leader might be replaced by a more aggressive up-and-coming company in the same industry. One of the best ways to evaluate market potential (and risk) is to observe how second-place companies in strong industries tend to emerge over time. Every leader in today's environment is at risk of being overtaken and replaced by another company in the future. Recognizing this emerging possibility far ahead of other investors gives you a tremendous advantage.

KEY POINT

It is the nature of the market to change. Perhaps the greatest risk investors face is overlooking this essential point.

Determining Risk Levels

Technical analysis is not restricted to the gathering of information to forecast the next big change in price; that is only one aspect. Expressed with greater breadth, technical analysis has the purpose of identifying opportunities *and* risk levels of various choices—the decision to buy, hold, or sell, as well as the selection of specific stocks to watch or to transact. To achieve this more sophisticated form of analysis, you need to concentrate on risk levels.

The most obvious sign that risk levels are changing is the change of price in a stock. Most people tend to think that when stocks fall in value, risk increases; and that when they rise, risk is lower and opportunity increases. Again, this type of segmentation of risk and reward is not productive. We all need to recognize that risk and reward always accompany one another. So it is more accurate to say that change in stock prices presents both opportunity and risk. A rising price level contains elements of risk as well as reward, for example. If a stock rises quickly, our experience reveals it is likely to suffer a correction. If prices rise while you do not hold shares, then you risk missing the opportunity to take part in the profit scenario. If your capital is tied up, you also miss the chance to shift money between stocks.

A falling price range also offers opportunity along with risk. A depressed price range is itself an opportunity, at times an exceptional one. Risk always accompanies a decision that might be hard to make, but the same argument applies to opportunity. So it is not whether prices rise or fall, but the fact that they change at all that presents the opportunity/risk picture.

With this argument in mind, resistance and support (along with other patterns in charting) are so critical. The support and resistance range of a stock—as long as the price remains within the defined area—shows that risk and opportunity are present only to the degree that a breakout might occur at some point in the future. Similarly, when the price range gradually emerges in one direction or the other, but without changing its breadth, that represents a type of change in risk and opportunity. And when the breakout is sudden and extreme, the risk and opportunity also are sudden and extreme.

KEY POINT

A change in price, upward or downward, represents a change both in risk and potential reward levels. The opportunity and danger are present on both sides.

Other signs of changing risk levels include:

- *Changes in levels of insider trading.* If a sudden increase in the volume of insider buy or sell transactions occurs, that also signifies a change in risk levels. (This indicator is of limited value because, under the law, insiders are restricted in the timing of their trades and profits; however, long-term insider trading watching can be beneficial.)

- *Cyclical change.* Remember that the market operates on cycles of supply and demand. Expressed simply, prices and price levels change because the supply and demand cycle is constantly moving. All of the elements and causes of price change go back to one form or another of supply and demand, those forces constantly tugging at one another and adjusting prices along the way. So as cycles rise and fall, risk levels change too.

- *Big fundamental changes.* Even very dedicated technicians cannot afford to ignore important changes in the fundamentals, and most of them avidly watch the financial changes of companies in which they are interested. Changes include mergers and acquisitions (especially those that eliminate competition through absorption), growth in sales and profits, dividend trends (especially the suspension of an expected dividend payment), and news that affects profitability (such as labor strikes or major lawsuits).

- *Changes in a company's position in its industry.* Remember, everything is subject to change, even the firmly held leadership position of a company within its industry. As a leader begins to lose its hold on leadership and other companies move up in the rankings, the entire risk/reward equation also begins to shift.

- *Changes in industry status.* Besides changes for individual companies, industry popularity comes and goes. Investors favor some industries over others at any given time, sometimes for good reasons and sometimes not. Whatever the cause, the illogic of the market rules, and the risk level for out-of-favor industries is greater (and potential rewards less) than for those "sweetheart" industries whose members can do no wrong in the eyes of their investors.

The Forms of Risk

Risk comes in many forms besides the well-known market risk. Below is a summary of the kinds of risk you need to be aware of as part of your technical analysis program.

Liquidity Risk (Cash)

The term *liquidity* has several different meanings, usually referring to the availability of cash. Liquidity is the combination of cash on hand or readily available, plus assets that can be converted to cash quickly. For example, you might have a savings account, several hundred dollars in a checking account, and a $3,000 loan owed to you and due on demand. Assuming the debt is collectible, all of these funds would be considered liquid. One variation of this idea in relation to the market is the condition in which capital is tied up. In other words, if you have all of your capital invested in a company whose stock has fallen, it sits there while you wait for a rebound, and meanwhile other stocks are rising spectacularly. Liquidity risk is accompanied by the uncertainty of whether to take a loss to move funds somewhere else, or to wait until matters change in your current portfolio. Liquidity risk often is demonstrated by the fact that investors tend to sell profitable stocks and take their profits; over time, they end up with a portfolio full of losers, having moved themselves out of the successful positions.

Liquidity is always a problem for investors, because unless you have unlimited funds, you need to think ahead carefully. If your capital is tied up completely, then you have none left to take advantage of new opportunities. And if you keep a portion out in reserve, then that part of your investment capital is left idle. Some investors use margin to borrow more money for future investing, a form of expanding capital. However, this greatly increases exposure to a different form of risk—interest rate risk.

When you borrow money to invest, you are required to pay interest for the time the loan is outstanding. Most investors should not use margin to increase their investment portfolios because the strategy is unsuitable for them. You are required to profit *more* just to repay interest; and if your portfolio loses value, you lose twice—once in the loss of capital and again because the borrowed money still has to be repaid.

The answer to the liquidity problem is patience. At times, you need to wait out a slow level of activity in your portfolio, so that you can time your sale while still meeting your goals. Otherwise, you violate the cardinal rule of investing: Buy low and sell high. Because of poor management of liquidity, some investors buy high and sell low—a difficult way to earn profits.

KEY POINT

Liquidity means more than how much cash you have around. It is more significant when studied in terms of what you have done with the investment capital available to you.

Liquidity Risk (Market)

Another form of liquidity refers to a ready market, to the ability to find buyers and sellers when you want to transact. The listed stocks in the U.S. market have a great deal of liquidity because the market has been set up to ensure order. Specialists act as buyers or sellers, depending on levels of supply and demand, ensuring that listed stocks find their market at all times. Other investments— such as limited partnerships, precious metals, collectibles, or real estate, for example—do not enjoy the same level of liquidity, making them more troubling in terms of liquidity.

The liquidity of the stock market is reflected in the ever-varying changes in prices. When a stock becomes unpopular, many sellers want to sell, so the stock price falls. And when a stock increases in popularity, more buyers want to buy, driving up the price. These are well-understood basics of supply and demand— as they operate within a liquid market.

In comparison, other markets are far from liquid. In the once-popular limited partnership market, based more on tax shelter considerations than on economics, there existed virtually no secondary market, a place for investors to sell their units at current market value. In fact, because these units often were inflated in value to begin with, their current market value often was nonexistent. The programs were designed to provide immediate tax shelter, so that no real future value could be expected. Thus, there was no demand and no secondary market. Remember, a secondary market is a reflection of continuing demand.

Another popular investment, real estate, continues to provide solid economic value but may also lack the liquidity investors desire. If the market is slow (meaning there are more sellers wanting to sell than there are buyers willing to buy), it will be difficult to sell property. Markets vary by region, so there is no way to forecast nationally what real estate markets will be like next month, even though many people assume that one region's situation reflects that of the entire country. The problems with real estate are primarily related to the liquidity—or lack thereof—in the market.

KEY POINT

Market liquidity in the stock market is very smooth, but this cannot always be said of other markets, where liquidity might be close to nonexistent.

Security Risk

As fundamentals change, stock values will reflect alterations in market value. These changes are not always reflected in stock prices right away. In fact, there is a tendency for the market to ignore fundamentals in the short term, and to pay more attention to the outcome of fundamentals relative to what analysts' forecasts said was going to happen. But pay attention to the fundamentals. In the long-term scheme of things, the fundamentals determine the entire profitability of your investment.

Most investors claim to follow the fundamentals, but if you listen carefully, you discover that few really do. They cite the Dow Jones Industrial Averages, analysts' estimates of future earnings, rumors about mergers, stock splits, and management changes—in other words, interesting details that have nothing to do with fundamentals. The truth is, most investors are distracted by rumor and technical indicators.

The stock chart is interesting and informative, but it reflects *price movement* only and not the fundamentals—position in the industry, sales, profits, and so forth. Even though most people know this, it is important to make the point, because it is easily forgotten. In the stock market, it is the actions rather than the stated beliefs of the investor that really tell you how that individual gets information. The security risk associated with misdirection is significant. If you believe in the fundamentals but react to nonfundamental information, for example, then you set yourself up for problems later.

Technical indicators are used properly to confirm (or to contradict) fundamental information. The technical signs tend to tell a lot about short-term and intermediate-term risk and likely stock price movement, whereas the fundamentals tend to be useful for longer-term decisions, like which stocks are good investments over many years.

KEY POINT

The fundamentals cannot be ignored. In the long term, they affect everything, even the technical indicators and, certainly, the stock's market value.

Diversification Risk

Common advice by market watchers and advisers is to "diversify," which usually means investing different percentages of your total capital in dissimilar investments. Some people believe that, because mutual funds diversify their portfolios over a broad range of stocks (and bonds in balanced funds), the diversification is achieved merely by buying shares in a fund with a positive track record. That might work. Depending on future performance, however, while the money you invest in a mutual fund has the advantage of compounded earnings, the overall record is not good. You might find that diversification by purchasing shares directly will work out more beneficially in the long run. Relying on a fund's management to do the analytical work for you is not necessarily wise.

In some respects, the advice to diversify is overstated, because situations do arise in which diversification is not necessary. The example above of investing in shares of a mutual fund is one such situation. The fund is diversified already so it is not wise nor necessary to purchase shares in several similarly designed funds. In fact, that increases your risk because it exposes you to different fund management. As we have already observed, the vast majority of mutual funds fail to achieve even an average rate of return. You would be better off to select one exceptionally well-managed fund (one that consistently falls within the 10 percent that exceed average market returns) and let your money work for you within that fund.

If you are managing your own portfolio, any significant diversification will be impractical with a limited amount of capital. You will save a lot in commission expenses by buying and selling in round lots, so buying odd lot shares is an expensive way to achieve a form of diversification that might not truly protect you against the risk you're trying to avoid.

Diversification is a fine idea when you have the capital available to invest in several different stocks, preferably in dissimilar industries. But when are just starting out, you are better off to

KEY POINT

It does pay to diversify, unless you choose poorly, in which case you end up only with a diversified range of poor performers. There is no substitute for diligent analysis and investigation.

pick one or two blue chip companies with exceptionally strong histories of stability, and allow your portfolio to build. Diversification might be a luxury at first.

Volatility Risk

Stocks vary among themselves in their degree of volatility, and the volatility of a single stock can change from time to time. Volatility, as measured by the trading range during the past 52 weeks, is a good test that can be applied consistently. You can track change within one stock, or you can compare two or more stocks, and it helps to have ease of access to the information (through daily stock listings). When a stock's volatility changes, there is a reason, and further investigation can help you determine whether your stance concerning that stock should change as well.

An interesting and informative application of volatility is to track it in comparison with PE. Because the PE reflects multiples of earnings as reflected in the current stock price, it is interesting to also compare changing PEs with changes in volatility levels. It is interesting to observe how low-PE stocks with relatively low volatility fare against high-PE stocks with relatively high volatility—not to mention the possible mixtures in between.

Measuring volatility in isolation is less revealing. Like any other indicator, it becomes more valuable when viewed in a larger context. It is not fair to conclude that high volatility always translates to high risk, although high volatility is one indication of a higher risk level. Different circumstances can create momentary volatility, including mergers, changes in product lines and mixes, changes in competitive stance, and overall market factors. A particular stock has to be reviewed on its own merits and in recognition that overall market forces might have a temporary affect on volatility.

In terms of on-going analysis, you cannot measure volatility only once and then leave it alone. Analysis becomes more interesting when previously established patterns change. So it is the change in volatility levels that tells you something is occurring.

KEY POINT

The test of volatility is an ever-changing test. Do not test once and expect a company's stock to maintain the same profile in terms of volatility or anything else.

Missed-Opportunity Risk

One form of risk often overlooked is the risk of failing to act, or of merely hesitating. The opportunities you miss might be as expensive as the mistakes you make by acting rashly or on poor advice. Missed opportunities, of course, also are bypassed risks—the flip side of the same idea.

Some particularly risk-averse people hesitate because they do not want to risk loss, so they pass up opportunities. This is a sign that they have not yet fully defined their goals or, of equal importance, their risk tolerance level. Because they are not sure about what is an acceptable level of risk, they simply do not act when they should.

Does missed opportunity translate to loss? Yes. Consider the extreme example, that of being so risk-averse that you do not invest any money at all. As a consequence, your capital is slowly eroded away by inflation, a form of specific loss. At the very least, the most conservative investor needs to identify investments with a rate of return sufficient to exceed the combined losses from taxes and inflation. Otherwise, the attempt to avoid all risk is guaranteed to generate a loss.

KEY POINT

The opportunities you miss could be as expensive as the mistakes you make by going for the wrong opportunities without enough information.

By defining goals and risk tolerance and then seeking out information, you will learn to overcome aversion to loss. That does not mean you will never have losses; it does mean that the risk of loss will be reduced to an acceptable level—a significant difference. The wise investor knows that losses will occur and hopes to arrange his portfolio so that the sum of gains is greater than (1) the sum of losses, (2) the effects of inflation, and (3) the expense of federal and state income taxes on dividends, interest, and capital gains.

Tax and Inflation Risk

The effect of taxes and inflation makes it necessary to earn a preliminary rate of return just to maintain the value of your capital. To evaluate the problem, consider the double effect of these problems. First, a portion of your profits are taken off the top for federal and state taxes. Second, the initial investment value of your capital is even further reduced by inflation. So an initial "decent" rate of return could end up being minimal, or you may even have an after-tax, after-inflation loss. With even a minimal rate of inflation, the risk of staying out of the market altogether represents gradual erosion of spending power.

The tax and inflation effect is significant. For example, let's assume that your marginal tax rate for federal and state taxes combined is 35 percent and that inflation is 2 percent. If your investments earn an 8 percent return, what does that really mean?

Gross return on $100 invested	$ 8.00
Less income taxes, 35 percent	– 2.80
Net return after taxes	$ 5.20
Less inflation, 2 percent	– .10
Net return after taxes and inflation	$ 5.10

Through this illustration, we see that an 8 percent gross return translates to a 5.1 percent net return after taxes and inflation. So a considerable chunk of your profits are eroded by these destructive forces. In some situations—where your earnings put you in the top bracket and where state income taxes are also steep—it is entirely likely that taxes alone will cut your investment profits in half.

This risk is not just a problem when you earn a profit; in fact, it points out the need to take some market risk. If you do not earn a fairly decent return on investments, the tax and inflation problem will erode your spending power over time. Inflation by itself is low these days, but even a small percentage of your spending power disappearing each year adds up over time. And what some people consider an acceptable rate of return actually is much lower after taxes.

KEY POINT

When taxes and inflation are considered together, you discover that you have to earn a strong initial return just to maintain your dollar's spending power.

Information Risk

You face the risk of information overload as well as that of using the wrong information. It is a handicap that so much information is available—so much, in fact, that you do not really know where to begin. So in such a situation how do you know whether the information you do select is valid and useful? Common sense and experience have to be employed to overcome the problem of too much information.

It is ironic that inexperienced investors believe their biggest problem with information will be finding it. The truth is that it requires considerable skill to develop a discerning eye so that you will know how to spend your time and energy. You need to sort through a mountain of potential information to get down to where the facts are hidden.

The problem is compounded by the Internet, where literally thousands of Web sites offer the promise of information, but most are come-on sites for subscriptions and services, most of which you do not need. The Web is a good source for free quotations, annual reports, articles, and other useful forms of free information. It is not advisable to pay for information found on the Web unless you already know it is something you need. For analysis, a single service like Value Line or Standard & Poor's probably provides you with everything you need in terms of raw data. For the rest, you can and should develop your own program.

Still, the sheer volume of information is tempting and distracting. It takes discipline to ignore it. Rather than responding to advertising hooks that get your attention, you can better use your time doing your own analysis, researching potential investment prospects, and monitoring your current portfolio.

KEY POINT

The problem is not a lack of information, but too much information—without the necessary distinction between what is valuable and what is junk.

Flawed Analysis Risk

With information in hand—even of the highest quality—you continue to face the risk that you might misinterpret the signals. This is a problem not only for the novice, but for the experienced technician as well. With so many possible outcomes, the future cannot be definitively understood with today's information, and all forecasting contains an element of guesswork. For this reason, you need confirming indicators for all signs before you draw conclusions. This is a basic rule for wise analysis.

Being mistaken in interpretation is common. It is far easier to see with hindsight what yesterday's signals meant, but not such an easy task for the present and the future. This is why it is so important to obtain independent confirmation before acting. No signal by itself should be taken as an absolute sign of the expected change. Chartists apply the technique continually.

When a chart signal (or pattern) indicates a particular change, such as a breakout from the established trading range, the indicated change is used only as a starting point. Other indicators are necessary as well. For example, you might discover that the company recently announced development of a new product line or acquisition of a competitor—moves that should improve its stock's market value. You could also discover that there is bad news, meaning the stock's price could be expected to fall.

The point is that analysis is not a precise science. The risk in undertaking analysis is that you might fall into the error of believing that certain signs are absolute, perhaps because those signs foretold change in the past. It is as though the signs themselves were constantly trying to deceive you. It is important, though, to remember that indicators do not have conscious intent. Even so, be sure to regard all information with a healthy degree of suspicion. Get independent confirmation before you act.

 KEY POINT

The need for confirmation is intrinsic to all forms of analysis.

Risk in Different Markets

Forms of risk are not universal to all markets. They change based on the characteristics of the investment itself, including the following.

Liquidity

The stock market is highly liquid, meaning that buyers have no trouble finding sellers, and vice versa. Other markets, however, do not contain the same degree of liquidity. Limited partnerships lack a secondary market except at deep discount; real estate might or might not have liquidity depending on market conditions; precious metal markets' liquidity depends on supply and current dealer policies; and collectibles have a notoriously poor liquidity because dealers sell at retail but offer to buy only at wholesale (meaning you need to double investment value just to break even).

Amount of Investment

The amount of capital invested often determines your liquidity. For example, in the real estate market, higher down payments make it easier to obtain financing. The higher the amount financed, the greater the buyer's risk. The financed amount is said to be leveraged, because the property was purchased with a small down payment. In concept, you could buy several properties by leveraging your capital; in practice, it is not so easy. The same arguments have to be applied to stocks. The more leverage used, the greater the risk (and potential reward).

Insurance

Some investments are insured, while others are not. For example, savings deposits are insured by one of several agencies, the best known being the Federal Deposit Insurance Corporation (FDIC) for banks. Savings and loan association and credit union accounts also are insured. But outside of the money market, it is practically impossible to insure your investment. The stock market offers no guarantees for stockholders, whereas bondholders have the pledge of a corporation (or government entity) and its assets that they will be repaid before stockholders in the worst case, complete liquidation. Bondholders do not have insurance in the traditional sense, but they do have a contractual guarantee, which is a form of "insurance" not enjoyed by stockholders.

The Dynamic Nature of Risk

Risk is an ever-changing reality in the market. It does not remain stationary, and you need to be aware that each analysis has to be revisited from time to time. Stocks, like the companies whose equity they represent, are dynamic; they change over time not only in price and perceived value, but in risk profile. A very volatile, unstable stock in today's market might be a rock of stability in five years.

If you invest for the long term, you need to check and recheck your portfolio to ensure that the risk profile is still suitable for you. Just as volatile stocks might settle down, some stable stocks by today's standards could be higher risks in the future, and for any number of reasons. The point is, change is a constant in the market—and is one of the features that makes it so interesting.

KEY POINT

Because everything changes in the market given enough time, you have to watch for changing risk profiles on long-term investments.

Risk and Reward

The relationship between risk and reward has been mentioned several times. But even among investors who know this, there is still a tendency to separate the two features. One may be aware only of the potential for reward in certain stocks and fearful of the risks in others, without recognizing that both are attributes of all stocks.

How does it work? It is an inescapable feature of all investments that risk and reward are linked together. Some would like the opportunities for profit without the risk, and consequently they tend to ignore the risk. Thus, they even might not be aware that some portion of their portfolio is invested in "aggressive" stocks, meaning the potential for reward is linked directly with equivalent higher risk. Other would-be investors, overly sensitive to losses, are aware only of the risks of certain investments. They are not aware of the reward, or they

> **KEY POINT**
> The fear and greed associated with a lot of investing is a reflection of overemphasis on risk or reward, without a concurrent understanding of how these features work together.

consider it inadequate, given the risk factor. As a result, they do not invest in some issues that might be completely appropriate for them.

In both cases, the way to solve the problem is through education. We gain experience from doing, often of the hardest kind. But we overcome the fear associated with risk and the greed associated with reward by gaining more information. Most people who miss opportunities because they fear risk would miss fewer such opportunities if they had more information. And most people who lose because they take uncalled for risks out of greed would be less likely to make the same mistakes if they better understood the nature of the market—including the relationship between risk and reward.

Speculation versus Long-Term Investing

Frequently preliminary definitions in investment profiles oversimplify the way the market works, using some broad generalizations, such as:

- Speculators take high risks, and long-term investors are conservative.
- Technical people take greater risks than fundamental investors.
- Speculation is bad and long-term investing is good.

Of course, none of these generalizations apply to everyone. An examination of each one makes the point.

Speculators often do go for higher-risk investments because they seek short-term profits of better-than-average size. Thus, with a greater tolerance for risk, they expose themselves to the risk side out of necessity. However, the activity of speculation itself does not make a person a shoot-from-the-hip investor. Many conservatives invest a small portion of their portfolio in speculative investments. Others use speculative devices in a conservative manner, such as writing covered call options against stock—a strategy that is itself conservative, although it generally is seen as exotic, high-risk, and very speculative.

KEY POINT

Exposure to higher risks does not always reflect a reckless approach. It might mean the individual has higher-than-average risk tolerance.

The second myth, that speculators take greater risks, is similarly flawed. By greater risk, one assumes an exposure to higher losses. But remember, speculators also are exposed to higher potential rewards. Ultimately, it is possible that speculation might result in higher returns and an on-balance lower risk factor. For example, if inflation is relatively high, what is the risk of extreme conservatism? Such a strategy ensures losses on a postinflation basis, and in such times a degree of speculation might be the more conservative strategy.

The third myth is a value judgment stating that speculation is unwise, bad, or poorly advised. That is not necessarily true. As

KEY POINT

Exposure to higher risks has another side: exposure to higher potential profits.

with all forms of investment strategy, you should know what you're doing before investing money, but this does not mean that speculation is bad for everyone, or that the more conservative choice of long-term growth stocks is good for everyone or in every case. The answer varies with the condition of the market, the nature of the investor, her age, the amount of money available, and each individual stock.

KEY POINT

Speculation is not "good" or "bad," but is one of many strategies that should be employed when the time is right.

Setting Risk Tolerance Standards

A final point to be made about risk is this: Everyone has his own risk tolerance level, a comfort zone for risk, and a personal requirement for minimal returns. Your personal level of risk tolerance will not be the same as someone else's, and it will not remain the same throughout your life. Several factors affect risk tolerance, including:

- Age
- Income level
- Marital status
- Capital available to invest
- Long-term goals
- Attitude toward markets
- Experience and knowledge

This is only a beginning list. Many other factors, including bias developed from your past experiences, also affect your risk tolerance level. For example, some people are irrationally opposed to home ownership, even though they have never owned a home, because someone they know once had a disastrous experience with buying a home. Even though much information is available to allay such fears, some people are not be able to see beyond their biases. The same is true in exotic markets, such as futures, options, or precious metals, all of which are highly specialized and require skill, experience, and mastery of terminology and rules.

> **KEY POINT**
>
> An array of factors, some not entirely rational, affect our perceptions. Thus, risk tolerance is different for everyone.

Your personal risk tolerance level for stocks—or for any investment, for that matter—depends on all of these features in your life. And your risk tolerance level will change as a result of many factors, such as:

- Marriage or divorce
- Death of a relative
- Birth of a child or children
- Buying a home
- Career changes (new job, termination, self-employment)
- Available money, which may change because of inheritance or unexpected catastrophic losses

The major life changes require reevaluation of your portfolio and of your risk tolerance levels. Some people make the mistake of analyzing their risk tolerance once, defining themselves, and then forgetting to perform the necessary maintenance over time. Just as the technical attributes of a particular stock change every year (not to mention every week in some cases), it is just as likely that as you grow, your attitude and risk tolerance will change, reflecting changing needs, such as your age to retirement, the size of the

KEY POINT

No matter how specifically you understand your risk tolerance today, it will probably be vastly different in only a few years because people, like everything else, change with time.

nest egg you have available, and even the kinds of things you plan to do with your life in the future.

It makes sense to understand your risk tolerance, a point many investors already understand. But of equal importance, it also is essential that you review this matter every few years and inspect your portfolio and your approach to investing with the new information in mind. When you consider how much your life has changed during the past five years, you can imagine how much farther it will evolve in the next five years.

CHAPTER 10

Combining Technical and Fundamental Analysis

A debate goes on constantly in the financial world between the fundamental and technical camps. Which approach is best? Which is the more reliable? The fundamental analyst points to the elegance of science, to the importance of the numbers, and complains that technical analysis is market voodoo. The technician argues back that financial information does not affect price immediately and that it is historical and backward-looking, and claims that charts and related indicators tell the whole story.

Neither side can lay claim to the entire truth, and each side have some degree of evidence to back up its claims. The fundamentals are precise, to a degree, because they are the result of careful and complex compilations of financial data, external audits, and internal controls. At the same time, there is a lot of room for interpretation, and management of big companies can employ techniques to control reported profits, at least to a degree. Through the process of accrual and deferral, corporate financial results can be manipulated while still conforming to the rules. So one criticism of the fundamentals could be that financial reporting is too easily open to interpretation.

Does this harm stockholders? Probably not. Management's job is seen by many as not so much to run a company—that can be done by middle executive officers—but to maintain and improve the market value of the common stock. If that is true, then skill-fully controlling reported sales and profits while ensuring the continued flow of dividends, keeping a positive public relations face on the company, while avoiding catastrophic lawsuits may be the real values and talents that top executives bring to the corporate world.

As complex and varied as the potential reporting methods are within accounting and auditing rules, the United States has a reliable and consistent record of honest reporting of corporate profits. As a general rule, investors can rely on the audited reports of corporate profits to be accurate, honest, and complete.

KEY POINT

The accounting rules give management a lot of latitude to manipulate what it reports. And this is not necessarily perceived as a problem.

As accounting rules can be interpreted differently by different people, so can technical indicators. It is true that technical indicators are forward-looking, while the fundamentals look backward. And because market perception is interested in potential more than history, the technical indicators draw more attention than the fundamental indicators. It is the ultimate irony of the investment world that most people claim to follow the fundamentals faithfully, but they really focus their attention on technical indicators—charts, rumors and gossip, and the biggest technical indicator of them all, the Dow Jones Industrial Average (DJIA).

Technical information is based on trading patterns visualized through charts, the inaccurate and distorted reporting in the DJIA, and an emphasis on short-term price changes. Even within inaccurate indicators some very valuable information can be found, notably in relation to trading patterns and the importance of support and resistance. Whether you subscribe to the Dow Theory or believe in the Random Walk Hypothesis, a lot can be learned from a study of technical information.

Because both fundamental and technical indicators provide some value—and because both have some blind spots—the most sensible approach is to make the best use of both. Thus, the concept of "technamental" analysis—the combined use of technical and fundamental information—is valuable to every investor.

The Approach That Makes Sense

Technamental analysis is an approach that gets around the ongoing debate. The question "Which is best, technical or fundamental analysis?" is, in fact, the wrong question. The point is, neither is purely right or wrong. Both offer something of value.

Seek the minority of indicators from each side that help you to make specific decisions about management of your own portfolio. The DJIA changes do not help you with the basic decisions you need to make about the stocks you own: buy, sell, hold, or flee. No change in the Dow can help you to make intelligent choices. For this reason alone, the DJIA is a useless management tool. It does provide an indication of the perception of the mood of the market. The question "Where is the market headed?" is really a useless numbers game. People like to predict where that magic Dow number will be next week, next month, or next year. But it is not the market, and it does not even come close to measuring the mood or sentiment of the market. It only measures the *perception* of the mood of the market. And as such, it might or might not reflect what is happening in the economy. So the DJIA is only an interesting and manipulated index; it provides no value.

To make effective use of technical and fundamental indicators, you will need to identify the few indicators from each side that make sense. Begin by following these five generalized rules:

1. *Forget about using the DJIA for anything.* The DJIA should not be followed too closely because it provides no useful information. Remembering that stock splits distort the

index by providing greater influence to some stocks and less to others, and also remembering that companies are added and removed from the list without specific explanation as to why, you should consider the DJIA to be highly suspect.

KEY POINT

The DJIA has been around for a long time. But even so, it really is not the market, and it really does not give you any information you can actually use.

2. *Review the essential information you need to anticipate change.* What do you really need to include in your analysis to properly anticipate what is likely to happen next? Certainly, all of the information you incorporate into your own program should relate specifically to the companies whose stock you have purchased (or are considering buying). And you should believe that your chosen indicators will have a direct impact on the stock's price. These are starting points.

KEY POINT

At a minimum, the information you decide to use should relate directly to the companies whose stock you own. Otherwise, what is the point?

3. *Limit the number of indicators you incorporate.* If you limit the number of indicators you select, you will be able to manage information well. Too many people believe that they will be more successful if they get more information. But it

makes sense to settle for less information of higher quality. So remember that more is not better. With too much data at your fingertips, you have no way to tell which indicators to follow, or what the collective information actually reveals.

KEY POINT

You could drown in excess information. You are better off with very little information of the greatest possible value.

4. *Identify primary and confirming indicators.* You will need to determine which indicators are to serve as your sources for primary information, and which ones you want to use for confirmation. For example, if you watch changes in price-earnings ratio (PE) and net profits, and confirm that information by tracking support and resistance levels, then you have the makings of a preliminary and basic program.

KEY POINT

All information needs to be confirmed by independent and separate means, so your program is best set up with primary and confirming indicators.

5. *Review and then review again. Learn from experience.* Some investors make mistakes of the same kind over and over. They do not learn from their experience. To succeed as an investor, you cannot realistically expect to never be wrong, or to make the right decisions every time. But you can monitor yourself and learn from the things that happen, positive as well as negative. It is the

negative experiences—especially the expensive ones—
that really teach us about investing, and these should be
watched and studied closely.

KEY POINT

As painful as they are, the expensive lessons are
the most valuable ones—if we actually learn them.

Using the Best from Both Sides

How do you create your own technamental program? To select
indicators most likely to help you in developing a personalized
program, follow these four general guidelines:

1. *Avoid highly obscure data.* A lot of so-called information,
   especially technical information, is really just a lot of complex formulas and excess analyses. The computer models of
   investing might be interesting to a college professor or math
   student, but for real-world investors these are useless and pre-
   tentious. What you really want is relatively simple: information clearly showing trends and averages, which can provide
   you some insight and a little bit of a jump on the market and
   can help you with the timing of your investment decisions.
   You cannot get that from a complex mathematical model of
   investment trends that confuses rather than enlightens.

KEY POINT

It seems that complexity is equated with quality
of information. In truth, though, truly valuable information is
elegantly simple, whereas complex, difficult to understand
information is more often a complete waste of time.

2. *Test indicators before using them.* Some people select indicators because they grasp how those indicators work—but they do not really know what information they provide or whether they are of any use. You need to find indicators that really show you how to estimate likely future outcomes, how to discriminate intelligently, and how to form sound judgments based on reason rather than emotion. So any indicator that appeals to you should be tested before it is used. Be skeptical of everything, and accept only what you believe is reliable.

KEY POINT

Be sure not just that you know how indicators function, but that you know they work—because you have already tested them for yourself.

3. *Use the financial press and subscription services.* A lot of good, basic information will be found in daily and weekly newspapers and magazines and in investment subscription services (such as ValueLine and Standard & Poor's subscription services). You will never be able to match the level and breadth of the information these services provide, which enables you to select what you consider valuable in your own program for portfolio management.

KEY POINT

Some of the best information is available through published sources and not from paid analysts or so-called financial planners, consultants, and other professionals.

4. *Do not accept something just because it is conventional.*
   The majority is usually wrong. So going along with the
   majority just because it is the majority will make you
   wrong just as often. As difficult as it is to follow this
   advice, prepare yourself to act as a contrarian, to go
   against the commonly held beliefs. Remember that many
   of the most strongly held beliefs about the market are
   wrong, such as the beliefs that mutual fund management
   is better than the typical investor at picking stocks; that
   the DJIA is "the market"; and that low-PE stocks are
   underachievers while high-PE stocks are "better" than the
   average. All of these ideas are demonstrably wrong, and
   yet even educated and experienced investors continue to
   believe in them faithfully.

KEY POINT

Never go along with the majority just because it is
comfortable. Give up a little comfort to be right more often.

Coordinating a Technamental Program

The most difficult task for any analyst—whether working pro-
fessionally on Wall Street or just trying to manage a personal
portfolio—is to make distinctions. The analyst is a discriminating

KEY POINT

Your worst enemy is information. Because there
is so much of it, it is difficult to find *good* information in the
big pile.

individual who must judge all information, quickly and with certainty. Why? Because by nature information itself requires judgment. There is so much information, a lot of which is junk or simply irrelevant, that one can become hopelessly lost in it if not able to be discriminating.

Coordination of this information is essential. As an investment management skill, coordination of information is an essential task everyone requires. It is a common error among investors to overlook the information overload problem and to become distracted by indicators and news that have absolutely nothing to do with their portfolio.

> ***Example:*** Let's say that you own 300 shares of a company whose stock has been inching upward over a six-month period. In recent days, however, the upward movement has stopped and virtually no change is occurring. Is this a signal or merely a pause? If a signal, what kind of signal is it? A lot of questions arise. In the search for information, you begin by studying a moving average chart, the most recent financial reports, a study of insider trading, an analysis of the PE, and a few other matters related directly to that corporation. Then you also find some interesting information about the most recent trends in the DJIA, showing changes in mutual fund investment patterns; charting patterns of the collective DJIA stocks and changes in the Dow Jones Utility Averages; and a study of new high/new low trends on the New York Stock Exchange. These unrelated indicators have absolutely nothing to do with the trading pattern of your stock and, probably, no effect on the stock's performance. Many investors track the market overall, but that still does not make unrelated information valuable in any sense of the word.

The tendency in the market is to pay attention to a lot of useless information because it is available, it sounds important, and it relates to overall market conditions. But there is no relationship to the actual stocks individual investors are trading. If you apply the logic of the market to other investment areas, you see the picture more clearly:

- You recently bought an investment property in a suburb and have rented it out. You read a newspaper article summarizing the latest findings, showing that national prices of residential properties have flattened out recently. In your community, a strong demand for housing has kept prices high. *Because real estate trends are always local, the national trends are meaningless in your situation.*
- You own several rare coins that you bought a number of years ago. Today, though, the market for coins is flat and the value has not gone up lately, so you are holding them as a long-term investment. You just read an article in a magazine stating that collectibles are going to be hot again next year. *A market glut does not go away suddenly, but has to be absorbed over many years; the prediction about the market sounds more like wishful thinking on the part of dealers than like sound investment advice.*

The examples make the point. Investments do not go through supply and demand cycles in tidy or predictable ways, but are more likely to react in complex ways. So the kinds of information available about stocks (or real estate or collectibles) is usually inaccurate for several reasons, including the following four:

1. *No one really knows what will happen.* The essential point to remember about information is that the majority of it forecasts in one form or another. Technical information is forward-looking, thus it is always predictive. In comparison, fundamental information is historical and more dependable, but tells us less about today and tomorrow.

KEY POINT

It would be refreshing to hear an expert say that no one can possibly know the future. Instead, we hear a lot of support for predictions, which are not right most of the time.

Remember that when it comes to market predictions, no
one knows what is going to happen. Informed opinions
might be informed, but they are still guesses.

2. *Many sources of information have vested interests.* One
   troubling fact about predictions is that the people making
   them often have something to sell. Consider the two
   examples of other markets just presented. Who makes
   predictions about trends in real estate? For this type of
   information, most journalists go to real estate professionals, the people who make their living earning commissions
   by selling real estate. Of course, these people want the
   market to be stronger, so their information is unavoidably
   biased. By the same argument, when journalists want to
   know what is going on in the collectibles market, they ask
   dealers, the people with more inventory than they can sell,
   who want to get more people interested in buying their
   products. Thus, the information cannot be trusted. The
   same is true in the stock market. The experts normally are
   brokers who earn commissions based on trading activity,
   service providers who sell subscriptions or consultation
   services, or analysts whose jobs depend on avid interest
   among investors in what will happen next.

KEY POINT

Whenever you hear a prediction, your first question should be "What does this person have to gain or lose
from the way that I react to this prediction?"

3. *Forecasting is attractive but inaccurate.* Everyone likes to
   predict the future. This is the great game of the market, and
   it often appears that people enjoy guessing the future more
   than making profits on their investments. The preoccupa-
   tion with the DJIA typifies this attitude. The market, generally speaking, wants to know where the Dow will go

next: Will it break the next level that is divisible by 1,000? Will it break the all-time point gain for a single day? Will it break the record for consecutive record high days? These are exciting prospects that are supposed to signify something important or meaningful, but they really do not. It is the prediction of the future that attracts people. The questions of a more technical nature are far less interesting, even though they are far more important.

KEY POINT

As much fun as it is to predict the future, you probably are more interested in making money—a point too often lost as the game proceeds.

4. *The majority of investors—and most information—is wrong most of the time.* We have said it before, but it bears repeating again: The majority is wrong most of the time. And the information generated for the majority as well as the opinions that result from it, also are wrong most of the time. As you view information, be aware of the danger in confident predictions of a direction for the Dow, realizing that it does not matter whether they are right or wrong. There is no way to actually know what will happen next, and the predictions are probably wrong. What you really need is the one piece of information you

KEY POINT

Relevant, accurate information is the most simple. And it is there. But so much else is out there too, it might be difficult to find without a lot of work.

cannot have: a scientifically accurate prediction about the immediate future price of the stock you own or are thinking of buying.

Indicators of Greatest Value

As a starting point, you should recognize that for you to properly manage your investments, any indicators should relate to them directly. Overall market indicators are interesting and do reflect perceptions and sentiment, but they do not help you to make your basic investment decisions. The real purpose in overall indicators might be to help analysts and journalists pontificate about what is going on in the market, but the big secret about all of that is that the information on which they depend is meaningless and vacant in terms of your individual portfolio.

These broad but useless indicators include mathematical trends, formulas, and equations about the overall market, all sentiment indicators of a general nature, the DJIA and other indexes, studies of records in high/low levels, changes in overall volume, and odd lot short sales, to name a few.

Of immediate value are all indicators that affect the market price and fundamental value of the company whose stock you own. These include, but are not limited to, the following 10 indicators:

1. *Fundamental information.* Even as a believer in technical analysis, you need to be aware of trends and changes in the fundamentals. Historical information, while backward-looking, provides you with a base for understanding the financial health of a corporation. Heed the wise advice that "history is a vast early warning system."*

2. *Insider trading trends.* The corporate insiders are prohibited by law from profiting from information not available to the investing public. Still, their own trading demonstrates a

---

*Norman Cousins, in *Saturday Review*, April 15, 1978.

greater depth and perception about the company than does that of the general public—it has to just by virtue of their position. Insiders may trade as part of an ongoing program, a sort of high-level payroll deduction; others might make decisions based on their own personal financial circumstances (e.g., impending retirement). But when sudden or unexpected reversals in a trend occur, insider trading trends are a valuable form of information.

3. *Industry-specific trends and changes.* The strength or relative strength of a company within its industry is dynamic. The competitive relationship of corporations within a single industry is like the building of a coral reef: a constant struggle for control over the territory whose changes might not be visible on a daily basis but will be significant and visible over time. Today's leaders are constantly at risk of replacement, and the other competitors are in constant expansion and building mode, always trying to overtake a greater percentage of the limited available market. As you see changes occurring, they might change your attitude toward any or all of the companies in that industry.

4. *Charting patterns of the individual company.* Be diligent in tracking the changes in price for the stocks you own, as well as for the stocks you are considering buying. It would be unwise to attempt to analyze each and every price change, so recognize that short-term trends do not provide you with important information. Use moving averages and limit your research and analysis to the major concepts of charting, especially support and resistance.

5. *The price-earnings ratio.* The PE is among the most interesting of indicators in that it combines technical information (price) and fundamental information (earnings). A couple of aspects of the PE warrant caution. First, the older the most recent financial information, the less reliable the PE. It is best to have a fresh financial report because things can change drastically in a fiscal quarter. Second, be aware that historically investors have

been wrong in how they perceive PEs. The general belief that higher-than-average PE stocks have greater-than-average potential has been consistently wrong in the past. And the perception that lower-than-average PE stocks have lower-than-average growth prospects also has been wrong. The opposite has been proven in long-term studies: higher PE stocks perform below the average, and lower-range PE stocks perform above the average. This demonstrates a tendency among investors to overestimate the growth potential of today's glamour stocks, and to underestimate the growth potential for the less exciting issues.

6. *Volatility of the stock.* The volatility, measured by the breadth of the trading range over the past year, is a key measurement of risk (and, of course, of potential reward). The greater the swing between annual high levels and low levels, the greater the volatility. This can be measured mathematically and studied through a moving average, or seen visually in a chart. As support and resistance levels change and trading range becomes redefined, the potential growth and risk aspects change as well. The study of emerging changes in volatility is a key form of analysis in studying stocks for intermediate-term and long-term growth.

7. *Volume in trading of the stock.* There is a direct relationship between volume and price. Volume changes often precede and anticipate price. For longer-term study of a stock, the development of a strong volume trend is very significant, and analysis of such changes might show either buying pressure (demand) or selling pressure (excess supply). Because the number of shares in a corporation is stable, changes in trading volume indicate changes in interest, and there is always a reason for such change.

8. *High/low record of the stock.* While overall market records for the number of new high price levels and new low price levels do not reveal anything of immediate

value, the opposite is true for individual stocks. When your stocks reach new high levels or new low levels (or when stocks you are watching do likewise), that can be taken as a signal to act. Considering that a new high represents the high over the past 52 weeks, it could signal that a peak has been reached and it is time to sell. As with all indicators, this phenomenom should be confirmed. And when stocks reach a new low, that could act as a buy signal, or it could signal a continuing deterioration in value. Again, these records are initial signs requiring further study, not definitive action.

9. *Major news of changes in the company.* As companies grow, they move into new markets, acquire smaller competitors or are merged with larger ones, change management, introduce new products and services, enter into litigation, suffer labor strikes, report extraordinary gains and losses due to changes in accounting methods, and make any number of other changes. All of these changes can affect the value of a company's stock, both in the perception of the market in the short term, and in reality in the long term. As an investor in a company, you will want to track company-specific changes, recognizing that not everything is reported in the financial statement or in the day-to-day changes in market price.

10. *Economic news affecting the company.* It would be impossible for a major corporation to operate without being affected by changes in the economy. Such changes affect all business enterprises. Changes in the money supply, interest rates, inflation, employment, and other indicators have varying effects on corporations, with some being more impacted than others. If an industry loses profits when interest rates rise, then any change in interest rates will have an understandable effect on profits *and* on stock price. If a company deals with an exceptionally large employment base, then a recession means a slow-down in production and heavy future layoffs, which also affect the company's stock value.

Developing Efficient Models for Analysis

No one indicator can possibly serve as the entire program for analysis of your stocks. It is the combination of indicators you develop for yourself—preferably limited to a few valuable tests—that makes your program efficient. Combinations of a few key indicators provides several important benefits, including three key ones:

1. *Confirmation.* The basis for all of your decisions should be discovery of what appears to be a signal and confirmation by an independent source. By using several dissimilar indicators, you build the confirmation requirement into your program.

2. *Variety of sources.* If all of your information were to come from one place, it would be suspect. You need information from a variety of sources, because in that way you will have an intricate means of confirmation as well as reliability. You need to ensure that your sources of information are varied enough so that you do not fall into the trap of depending on one source too much.

3. *Form of information.* You cannot depend solely on any one form of information, such as purely financial, charting, or volume trends. You need all of these. The more forms of information you have available, the better. Of course, you still need to limit the degree of information processing you have to go through, to discriminate in an attempt to find meaningful information rather than a mere quantity, and to constantly refresh and review your entire program.

The process of technical analysis is not limited to identifying the sources of information you use, confirming it, and then making automatic decisions about buying, selling, or holding. It also requires studying many elements, reviewing with an open mind what you might include or reject, and being willing to make changes, to try something new, or to modify your plans according to the experience of analysis itself. Successful investing is not a general process with one method that works for everyone. Given the kinds of stocks you buy, your personal goals, your risk tolerance, and your attitude toward each type of indicator, you will need to develop your own personalized analysis program— and then review it and change it from time to time.

Technical analysis, like so many other aspects of investing, is a process that you move through, not one that you simply learn and then do in the same way forever. Realizing that no one has the answers makes investing more interesting. It also makes it more challenging and risky, but potentially more profitable in the future. If it were easy to find a magical answer to all investing decisions, it would not be as rewarding as beating the odds to earn a short-term profit or just build equity over many years.

Appendix—Technical Formulas

Breadth Advance/Decline Indicator

$$\frac{(A1 \ldots A10) \div 10}{(A1 \ldots A10 + D1 \ldots D10) \div 10} = B$$

$$
\begin{array}{rcl}
A & = & \text{advancing issues} \\
D & = & \text{declining issues} \\
B & = & \text{breadth index} \\
1 \ldots 10 & = & \text{days in the moving average}
\end{array}
$$

Volatility

$$\frac{\text{annual high} - \text{annual low}}{\text{annual low}} = \text{volatility}\%$$

Mutual Funds Cash/Assets Ratio

$$\frac{\text{cash}}{\text{total assets}} = \text{ratio}$$

New High/New Low Ratio

$$\frac{\text{number of new high issues}}{\text{number of new low issues}} = \text{ratio}$$

Advance—Decline Ratio

$$\frac{\text{number of advancing issues}}{\text{number of declining issues}} \quad = \quad \text{ratio}$$

Large Block Ratio

$$\frac{\text{large block volume}}{\text{total volume}} \quad = \quad \text{ratio}$$

Short Interest Ratio

$$\frac{\text{number of shares sold short}}{\text{total volume traded}} \quad = \quad \text{ratio}$$

GLOSSARY

absolute breadth index A factor representing the difference between the number of advancing issues and the number of declining issues. The positive or negative value is not considered important, because this index measures the degree of change.

advance/decline line The daily net difference between advancing and declining issues, added to or subtracted from the previous day's running total.

advance/decline ratio A comparison between the number of advancing and declining issues, expressed in the form of a decimal or a percentage.

bar chart A chart that shows daily trading ranges with vertical lines representing the ranges, and a horizontal representation of time.

breadth advance/decline indicator A study that compares the total number of advancing issues to the total number of declining issues.

breadth of the market A description of the strength of a movement, based on the number of issues involved. For example, a rally can be quantified by the number of advancing issues.

breakaway gap A gap series that moves into territory with no near-term price activity. If the gap is not "filled" with price activity consolidating new and prior ranges within a short time—a few days—this is a very strong signal that a bull trend is underway (for rising gaps) or that a bear trend is underway (for falling gaps).

breakout A move in price range extends the range above the resistance level or below the support level.

broadening formation The charted pattern that emerges when prices change over time so that trading expands in a vertical range.

closing-price bar chart A popular stock chart showing a vertical bar to represent each day's trading range and a horizontal tick to show the closing price.

common gap A commonly occuring minor gap between trading ranges characterized by trading within established ranges and not signaling a change in previously established patterns.

confidence index A widely followed and popular indicator developed by *Barron's* in 1932. It is the result of dividing the average yield of high-grade bonds by the average yield of intermediate-grade bonds.

confirmation Support or verification based on one or more indicators of what is reflected on another indicator, a requirement for proper systematic use of technical analysis.

contrarian An investor whose approach to the market is to assume that the majority is wrong most of the time, and who therefore acts in a manner contrary to the most commonly held beliefs at the time.

cumulative volume index The net difference between upside and downside volume.

cycle The predictable pattern of change in markets and the economy. The cycle changes as levels of supply and demand vary. In the stock market, greater demand causes prices to rise and excess of supply makes prices fall.

diversification The process of spreading risk among different investments, industries, or strategies, so that no single event affects the entire portfolio; a classification of risk described as exposure to events that can be mitigated by investing capital in dissimilar ways.

double bottom A formation that occurs when a stock's price falls to form double dips with a price rise in between, often showing that a strong downward trend is about to reverse.

double top A formation that occurs when a stock's price rises to form double peaks with a valley in between, often showing that a strong upward trend is about to reverse.

downside volume The total volume of trading in stocks that have lost value.

Dow Theory A theory founded on the observations of Charles Dow, based on the idea that market trends can be tracked and anticipated with the use of an index, and that certain rules apply in the recognition of emerging trading patterns.

efficient market theory A theory that the current stock price reflects all currently known public information about a particular company and its stock.

exhaustion gap A relatively small gap in the established direction, to be followed shortly by a reversal of direction.

flags A chart pattern that occurs when prices rise or fall together, creating rising or falling parallelgrams that illustrate the trading range.

fundamental analysis The study of recent and historical financial results of a corporation for the purpose of forecasting future investment value.

gap A pattern in which the trading ranges of two consecutive days contain a gap between one day's high price and the other day's low price.

head and shoulders A trading pattern consisting of three upward price surges: the first and third are the shoulders and the middle—the highest of the three—represents the head.

insider An individual with the opportunity to have more information about a company than the average investor, such as an executive, a key employee, a member of the board of directors, or a major stockholder.

insider buy or sell A transaction in a company's stock by an insider, such as an officer, key executive, or major stockholder.

institutional investor An investor whose capital is the combined capital of many stockholders or subscribers. The mutual fund is a typical institutional investor; other examples include pension plans and insurance companies.

inverse head and shoulders An upside-down head and shoulders trading pattern characterized by three downward trends: the first and third represent the shoulders and the middle dip—the lowest range—represents the head.

large block ratio The percentage derived by dividing the trading volume of large blocks by the total volume on the exchange.

margin The difference between a stock's market value and the amount paid; the amount loaned to a stock purchaser by a brokerage firm.

margin debt The amount of money borrowed by investors and brokers, with securities left on account as collateral.

market risk The general risk that prices of stocks will move in a direction other than that desired and, in addition, a range of related risks associated with opportunity, diversification, liquidity, and inflation.

members People who are able to buy or sell on the floor of the exchange, either for their own accounts or for the accounts of others.

members' short index A measurement of members' short trading trends, used to recognize when members go against the majority.

misery index A calculation using three separate economic statistics: prime rate, inflation rate and unemployment rate.

moving average A technique used for the analysis of trends in which an established number of periods are averaged, the effect being to smooth out exceptionally wide swings and to show more generally how a trend is developing. Moving averages also may be weighted in several ways to provide greater emphasis to the latest information.

mutual funds cash/assets ratio A ratio that shows changes in the trend among large institutional investors to invest capital or to hold out until changes occur in the market.

new high/new low ratio A ratio derived by dividing the new highs by the new lows, reported in the form of a percentage.

number of advancing issues The total number of stocks whose price rose.

number of declining issues The total number of stocks whose price fell.

odd lots Lots of stock of less than 100 shares.

odd lot short indicator A widely followed indicator that is based on trends among odd lot traders selling short, based on the belief that investors who trade in odd lots are inexperienced and usually are wrong.

pennants A chart pattern that occurs when price ranges narrow to create a pennant-shaped, narrowing trading range.

price-earnings ratio (PE) A comparison between a company's current market price and its earnings per share as of the latest financial report.

Random Walk Hypothesis A market theory that states that all price movement is the result of supply and demand in varying degrees of knowledge (some well informed, other badly informed), and that, as a consequence, all price change is random.

range The breadth of trading: the difference between the high and low prices that a stock sells for during a period of time. The range is further distinguished by its resistance level (top) and support level (bottom).

resistance The price or price range representing the highest price a stock is likely to reach under current conditions; the top of the trading range.

reversal day A pattern in which a day's trend opposes the previously established trend.

round lots Lots of stock of a number of shares divisible by 100.

runaway gap An acceleration in the breakaway pattern.

sentiment indicators Indicators meant to gauge the mood of the market

short interest ratio The number of shares sold short divided by total volume during the same period.

short sale A transaction in which stock is sold in an opening transaction, in the belief that the market price will fall and with the intention of closing the position with a purchase at a lower price.

simple bar chart A bar chart showing trading in a stock, with each day's vertical bar representing the full trading range during that day.

spike A top of a trading range that is considerably higher than that of the day before or after (*spike high*), or a bottom of a trading range that is considerably lower than that of the surrounding days (*spike low*).

supply and demand The two forces at work in the market that cause changes in prices and characterize the constant change in trading cycles. Levels of supply and demand determine the market price of stocks.

support The price or price range representing the lowest price a stock is likely to reach under current conditions; the bottom of the trading range.

technamental analysis The combined use of technical and fundamental information.

technical analysis The study of stock prices and related matters, involving analysis of recent and historical price trends and cycles and factors beyond stock price, such as dividend payments, trading volume, index trends, industry group trends and popularity, and volatility of a stock.

trading range The price range in which a stock trades during a specified period of time, defined as all prices in between a high price and a low price.

trend A movement in a stock's price, volume, or other studied matter, in which an overall tendency or direction is established and can be identified through the use of moving averages and analysis.

triangle A trading trend in which the trading range narrows in a diminishing pattern.

upside/downside volume line A comparison between the volume in stocks rising in value and the volume of stocks falling in value.

upside volume The total trading volume in stocks that have risen in value.

volatility The relative degree of tendency in a stock's price to swing between a range of high-to-low prices.

wedge A trading pattern showing a narrowing in the trading range.

weighted moving average A moving average in which some data are given greater weight than others, often from the most recent days in a field.

INDEX